THE RED SLIDE

To my wife, Darija, whose patience and support makes the hardest things in life possible.

To my sons, Angelo and Rafael, that your life will be filled with opportunity and joy if you seek it out.

PREFACE

For many leaders the journey to where they came to be involved many colourful stories. Most of them contain persistence and resistance on their journey. Picture a upward climb on a slippery slide. The reason this book was written was to help new leaders that have started their journey and to help them avoid many of the mistakes that others have made.

I planned this book for years, accumulating knowledge, ideas, conversations and observations from vast areas of life and business. The tough part was putting it all together to make a book which paints where leadership needs to go in the future. The purpose was not to have a comprehensive piece of literature that would take precious time, but rather to get to the point and move on. I want the reader to learn and understand, but most of all apply the knowledge in their everyday lives as a leader.

There is no special way of reading this book, all that is important is that in the end, your leadership and they way you conduct yourself is in anyway is improved. If that is the case then the book and the time it took to write and research would have paid off.

CONTENTS

INTRODUCTION

When we were kids we did a lot to play around. I suppose all of us went to the local playground where there were swings and monkey bars and most of all slides. It was a good exercise and having fun.

We have seen and have experienced many kids trying to climb the slide from the bottom up, not using the stairs around back of the slide. The slippery contraption makes it difficult to grab hold and climb, often the feet slipping every time we take a step froward we slide a bit down.

This red slide, can be seen in leading groups of people whether they be large or small. This metaphor for leading is what happens when leaders are faced with a red slide journey. We all encounter this, the difference is are we prepared with the knowledge and tools to climb a slippery slope of people leadership.

For the sake of argument, not all leaders will face a uphill climb in their careers of lives, for the rest of us, however, we are caught in a steep slide of uphill battles. These situations can be managed and seen as well as planned for if we arm ourselves properly for what is to come. How much easier would it be if someone threw a rope from the top of the slide so that we can anchor ourselves and pull to get to the top. This rope is this book. To anchor you into what you need to have to be a effective leader.

The Red Slide

Leading has become a task that many are avoiding, they dabble in it at the beginning only to give up after momentary defeats. Effective leading is understanding that many circumstances that befall a leader are learning opportunities, used for additional support in their final outcome.

The defeat that you might be going through is part of the leadership learning cycle. You learn and try, even failing at some point. The understanding of where these failures come from are often associated with personal awareness, cultural trends, people psychology and lack of personal commitments.

Your goal is not to dabble in politics of organizational life (even if they are unavoidable), or play power games with peers or even influential tactics with your superiors. Your aim should be of personal commitment to excellence in leading. The major difference in leadership that excels and one that doesn't is in the pursuit of doing small things in a excellent way.

To get to this point, it is in the rigorous effort to listen to others and focus on their problems not your own. Correcting your behaviour while building relationships will get you and your group of followers to the top of the red slide.

LEADING YOUR OWN WAY

While it is relatively not important what scientific style you are you should be aware of the styles that you want to use more and those that you want less of. Leadership is often looked at the eye of the beholder and as such it has been classified into various forms.

The style that most suits you and your personality will ultimately determine how you succeed with others. It is important to determine this and then work on perfecting a style that you need. All styles are not created equal and sometimes you need to adjust to the situation. If someone gave you a bunch of ingredients to cook something, without proper training and education you would probably make a dish that is not that good. With enough experimentation of those given ingredients you could probably with enough time make a particularly tasty dish with not using everything that was handed to you. Keep this in mind as sometime leading is not using everything in your arsenal.

"Lead me, follow me, or get out of my way"—General George Patton

This experimentation has been studied and identified that leadership is classified under two areas: relationships and tasks. Task behaviours make sure that the job gets done. Relationship behaviours ensures that everyone feels comfortable with each other, themselves and the situation they are in. This chapter will be useful to you

7

in identifying what style of leadership is needed. Furthermore, as a rule in leadership as you can be sure that no two leaders are alike but that they do use similar styles.

With the introduction of styles we need to dive deeper into understanding them. Stogdill in 1974 made the leadership behaviour description questionnaire. The purpose of this was to identify behaviours from all walks of life and profession that leaders would exhibit. This questionnaire made it possible to learn more about leading and following.

This is the essence of defining leadership, who follows? Who leads? Your purpose is to provide structure for your followers and then to nurture them going forward. Stogdill's research is unique in that It identified that leaders with these behaviours do not intersect but follow their own path. One leader might be more inclined to show compassionate behaviour while low on providing structure and vice versa. The lines might come closer together but never touch as each personality will be inclined to be more of one area than the other. This is also a reason why defining a leader or the term leadership is so hard.

It is not the genetic disposition of what you are, being either more of a relation people approach or a results driven approach, which we will get at soon enough it is having the mindset to identify which one we should be using that will make you successful.

In our world now, the meaning of success is subjective and knowing which style to use successfully is the same. The managerial grid ® which was made by Blake and Mouton, describes five leadership styles and will help you figure out which one to use. 1) authority-compliance. 2) country-club management. 3) impoverished management. 4) middle of the road management. 5) team management. I will build on what they have described and we will make our own leadership grid of what we need to know from these five styles as leaders.

1. We need this done Leadership: You will encounter tasks and/or projects that have unbelievably ludicrous demands. Time demands, cost demands, people demands, and on top of it all you are responsible for delivery. You should look at these situations as a constantly moving drill boring a hole into the wall. You are at the head of the drill and you need to get that hole pierced, you need not sugar coat this project as your people will see that you are the one leading the drilling and they must get along for the ride.

2. Limp leadership: Free from the pressure to perform is similar to a vacation to disneyland. Not that I think Disneyland as a soft mushy type of place, however, this style is best used when there have been incidents involving much human negativity. Creating a positive environment is key, where the production needs to keep going but you want people to get along,

at least for the time being. Comforting, eager to help, agreeable, and open door are the key terms here. Elements of negativity will eliminate any results your worked hard for.

3. Surrendered Leadership: This leader has resigned and does not care for results or for the people. They are there to collect a paycheque until someone finds out and puts them out of their misery. Avoid the temptation to give in.

4. Half and Half Leadership: Not emphasizing too much on people and not too much on tasks. They look for the moderation in everything, "don't rock the boat" they say. They still want everyone to get along and get stuff done, however, they do just enough. They are not pushers.

5. Troupe Leadership: this is the most powerful form a leader can take. Both tasks and relationships are strong. Everything in this leader is poised to endure stress and resolve people issues through collaboration and understanding all the while moving ahead with results. This

"Leadership is lifting a person's vision to high sights, the raising of a persons performance to a higher standard, the building of a personality beyond its normal limitations" —Peter Drucker

leader has a open minded attitude towards changes that might happen and ideas that his team members bring him.

Something to keep in mind when learning your style. Be careful that you don't get caught in the hubbub of your own train of thought. You should be able to feel how people are reacting to you. Why feel? It is important to notice if your current style is not working, you might need to change something fast. The master swordsman Miyamoto Musashi once said, "Perceive that which cannot be seen with the eye.". It is the atmosphere when you walk into the room. If you eat your lunch standing up, do you expect everyone else to do the same? These cue's will show in your followers perceptions of you and what you do.Learning what ticks you off is as important as learning about what ticks others off.

Self awareness is evident in historical examples such as in the Qin dynasty. There lived a man called Shang Yang. He was a statesman who reformed much of what the country was doing at the time, he is also responsible for successfully solidifying the Qin Dynasty through his philosophy. He created two theories while in office: Ding Fa (improving standards) and Yi Min (everyone to be treated equally). This leadership style is similar to what leaders nowadays are trying to achieve. Call it eternal opportunities to solve problems.

Shang Yang wanted success in the country more than anything else, and he influenced many in order to get his goals. Punishing those that did not report crimes, and rewarding military personnel based on status and merit. He also pushed for cultivation of agriculture over the luxury markets at the time. He made China successful by his aggressive style of change leadership. The irony in this example is that his death inflicted by the new King Huiwen, (Shang Yang got caught by one of his own laws), the inn keeper refused to give him a room without proper identification, which the punishment was imprisonment. The new king kept many of the laws Shang Yang implemented, they however, were so effective that the creator ended up at the business end of them.

Shang Yang's story is important because it tells us the importance of looking ahead for the good of the country (organization/team) and ourselves. If our efforts are for the improvement of the government and we are looking for lasting success we must be prepared for the backlash of people who do not want this. Shang Yang made many enemies in his quest to improve China and he ultimately paid the price in the end. Adjust your style or risk becoming a victim from others and your own success.

Confidence

Confidence is the ability of individuals to see and believe that they possess the skills and talents to execute certain actions, both mental and physical. Confidence doesn't stop there, it involves the training of the mind and its strengthening or weakening through our experiences. Psychologists have studied confidence as a point of reference for happiness in people. The more confidence you have the happier you will be. The famous Austrian psychologist Alfred Adler based his work on the ability for people to work in the realms of success or failure,which stems from their confidence in their skills. High level positions are given to confident leaders.

The subjective nature of confidence involves the honesty that is involved from and how we perceive ourselves, regardless of external intervention. This characteristic of leadership comes from within the individual. It would be difficult if not impossible to try and convince someone else to be confident in what they are doing, if they themselves are not involved in making that decision. It is this reason leadership is hard. We should not try to convince others to be confident but rather we should display confidence ourselves and from there they can see what confidence brings. Its almost a show and not tell game.

> "Anyone can hold the helm when the sea is calm."— Publilius Syrus

The Carthaginian military commander, Hannibal (247BC) would be histories great example of someone who portrayed confidence to everyone around him friend or foe. Imagine someone   (like Hannibal) challenging the greatest power on earth (Rome) and even occupying large portions of Italy for more than 15 years. This was at a time when everyone was terrified to utter a bad word about Rome. To have such power within yourself to control what you believe and what you do not believe is undeniable. It came to the point where Roman legions would all together avoid battle with Hannibal because of the reputation he had built for himself.

Building this reputation is hard. If we could imagine us for a second, that we are Hannibal. Before even setting foot on Roman territory what would our internal dialogue be? I am going to take on the most advanced, highest funded, optimally trained army and power on earth? Can I do it? This would be at the same level as if a small business owner would go up against a giant such as Google or Microsoft and take majority of their customers within a few short years. Having this internal ability and absence of fear, that even if I fail I have succeeded, is what you should strive for.

To master this internal ability we must practice. The examples that are given to us from history on confidence are part of what psychologists describe as a 'state of being'. This state is either positive or negative. Your leadership capabilities depend on and are expressed from this state. The internal dialogue that you experience is your subconscious trying to convince you on why you cannot do something based on your life experiences. Hard economic times could cause you to be more passive in making risky investments, or a health related issue can make you squeamish with regards to adventure. Evidence that you gathered throughout your life will ultimately impede confidence as you will rationalize with what others have done and said. This is the end of the process, where the influence of others have taken over your thoughts and others are doing the thinking for you.

Confidence without rationalization is foolishness, overconfidence without merit or cause will make enemies and resentment towards you. You must have accurate information in order to retain correct confidence. In your leadership role you will ultimately discern what you will be more and what less confident on. There are many leaders that end up being annoying and even silly as they did not gather enough facts to accurately push their plans through, and they end up looking foolish. Overconfidence makes us lazy.

Athletes are examples of how confidence can drive a result. Confidence can be swayed within seconds and that is why it is important for you as a leader to understand it. Knowing when your confidence is going to fall before it does is the goal you are looking for. Call it intuition or meta cognition. When you have a client that suddenly rejects all your hard work and goes with someone else, are you going to quit your job or blame yourself for the whole situation? Of course not. There are too many variables involved in this. Move on with your life and grab the next client. All athletes fail and fall, but they all get back up.

"A good general not only see the way to victory, he also knows when victory is impossible"— Polybius

Setback and failure are good and are excellent teachers. Experience provides us the limits of what can and should be done (notice I didn't say cant be done). There are situations where we believe that we have the abilities to do a job or event, however, at the time we lack the resources. Much like Hannibal we should not assume that down the road we will have resources thrown at us, rather we should evaluate the land or business and see if we can use what is there already. This is experienced confidence, when we know our limits and choose consciously to take certain actions instead of diving into the unknown. This is built from failure which is the mortar to keep building a poised attitude.

Confidence is a choice where attitude is part of this choice. We will talk about attitude later on, but you should know that these two pieces fit into the role of the leader. They are linked, the sense that something can be accomplished is part of attitude and boosts our confidence. Look at attitude as subjective data and confidence as objective data, together they can work on solutions. Confidence in this sense is self awareness and reflection of daily interactions.

We should look at a example of confidence and self awareness. Trained by one of histories greatest thinkers, Aristotle, motivated by a ambitious father, Philip of Macedon and counselled by his mother to predestined greatness, Alexander, later known as Alexander the great had the recipe for success. At 14 he was a Macedonian warrior, at 18 became general and at 20 king. It was not his pedigree that made him this successful but his confidence in his abilities. This enables a person to push himself over what others would think god like.

The fascination of Alexander with us is to know how is it possible to conquer the known world in such a short time period in the same venture by a twenty year old. All this at a time where war was the pass time, everyone was studying it and everyone was edging to take the other weaker sides land and territory. Alexander was certainly not bred for war, however, he was influenced by his surroundings. The only strategic advantage that Alexander has had instead of you would be that he was born into royalty. This is trivial in comparison to the achievements that he made, and in comparing others born in the same way we see that many if not all become complacent to their luxurious lifestyles living off the fruits of their fathers. Not Alexander, and not you.

Most of what we know now of Alexander was written by historians long after his death. It would have been interesting to know the dialogue of a young man in a country that was about to be attacked from all sides following the assassination of his father Philip. What would a teenager today say to a country now? Our teenagers and young adults are flopping around bars and playing video games, maybe the times then were focused around war instead of instant gratification. Remember that confidence is a choice that must be built. Whatever the conversations were, they must have had thoughts for survival and succession, of which to have these you must be sure of yourself and of the people you lead. Something Macedonia desperately needed.

Alexander's mother, Olympias was the inspiration that the young boy went to. Her sole purpose for Alexander was to embed in him the confidence to take over the known world (literally). We also have these forms of Olympias in our lives, our parents, mentors, coaches and more importantly ourselves. We should be the Olympias in our own minds, knowing that no matter what goes wrong we are destined for greatness. Even when our bosses are unresponsive to our needs and our negotiations do not go as planned we must pursue our final destination. This was the unconscious driving force for Alexander and his achievements. Being absolutely ruthless on your inabilities and weaknesses is what you and Olympias of your mind should be doing as they did for the success of Alexander.

> **"A man who wants to lead the orchestra must turn his back to the crowd"**—Max Lucado

Everything we read about in that time about Alexander oozes poise. Another example was from the trader from Thessaly who brought king Philip a horse to buy, strong and fast with a heavy price tag. The horse, however, proved to be useless as it was too wild and could not be tamed. King Philip enraged that the trader was trying to trick him, ordered him and the horse away, Alexander seeing this decided to step in a challenge the king of riding a beast such as this. Successfully mounting and galloping away with the horse Alexander proved to the King and all who were watching that he was not going to take failure as a option. Alexander would ride this horse, Bucephalus, into the conquering of the Persian empire and more.

Future expectation and vision will need to mingle with confidence. You don't care that the world is out to get you, you are biding your time for when you are ready, and when you are you will overcome anything in your path. Confidence is a true measure of a leaders capability, as it is the hardest to get. Too many outside influences interfere with our decision making abilities and taint our levels of confidence. Failure is the product of a defeating mindset and failure is common, confidence destroys any doubt that you are destined for action and success and without self respect it is a hard thing to come by.

What confidence does, is solidifies your abilities as the leader of the group, after all without confidence you probably wouldn't be the leader. You are the man for the job and the others will have to wait for you to retire or move onto greater things for them to take your seat. People will have no choice but to see what you are doing and where you are taking them. Self assurance building is knowing that nothing is forever, and the temporary setbacks that you encounter are only learning pieces that you assess and move on with.

Attitude
The leaders attitude reflects in their confidence and self esteem.

If I asked you if you would rather win $5,000 now or $8,000 a year from now what would you answer?

If you answered $5000 now, then you are certainly impatient. What does this have to do with attitude? Or even confidence? Patience is a attitude and then it is needed in confidence. Often when we hurry to the goal we are compensating for something, usually subconsciously we think that we might falter if we take our time, that time is against us and that we must finish this now or it'll be too late. Knowing time limits will adjust your attitude and confidence. It is easier said than done, because time limits are set by others rarely ourselves.

"Educations is the mother of leadership"— Wendell Willkie

Time and patience is part of your mental makeup in how well you cope with stress, and the unknown. If you think that you will fail, guess what you probably will. Attitude and patience seem to be connected as we have seen the $5000 might have some urgency connected to it, you might have debts to pay now and don't really know what the future will hold for you in a year. Why risk it, take the money now. If we think about a person who displays confidence, would we notice that they are impatient? Probably not, at least not in the long term of things. They think strategically.

Patience is connected to confidence as apples are to the apple tree. The tree is patience and the apples are confidence and it is a attitude that is practiced. The way we take our time to think things through and not rush, shows that we know where we stand mentally and are able to delay gratification. We trust ourselves that not rushing to conclusions or hasty decisions will produce better results than if we reacted right away without looking at all the options. Patience is a virtue truly echoes in confident leaders.

Lets test another example for attitude and patience.

Your company invested $1 million dollars in a project that was expected to generate a revenue of $5 million after the first year. The year went by and it got nothing. Something that is all too common and nerve wrecking.

You now get the news that another investment opportunity in that same project has come. There is a 20% probability that it will succeed and yield $10 million dollars in a year and nothing after. There is also a 80% chance that the project will give you nothing. How much will you be willing to invest now?

If you replied anywhere between $1 million or more dollars then you are willing to overpay in order to save the project of a "sure loss". Your attitude towards risk (and the stress and confidence associated) on yourself and your groups should be seen as, do or die. How far are you willing to go to get the result you hoped for, how much pain can you take before breaking. Most risk adverse individuals stop after the first loss and move on. Leadership is not for those who stop at the first sign of failure. They reassess the risks and adjust their leadership. Having a clear head will help you do this.

Many things might test your attitude and patience in whatever it is you are doing. This testing is called experience. Experience is the most valuable test as it influences you on the personal level. You know you shouldn't touch a hot stove as it will burn your finger, an experience that was painful and your attitude towards a hot stove is to be careful. A failed team member who recently quit to work somewhere else might make you hesitate in hiring someone who is of similar background and profile.

Leadership is much the same, if you attitude towards a hostile and arrogant member of the team is that they cannot be controlled or talked to, then the result will be just that. You perception and what you tell yourself concludes the result of your-self talk.   You can talk to anyone about anything if you have the data and the right attitude backed by patience and self assurance.

"It is absurd that a man should rule others, who cannot rule himself."— Latin Proverb

In a research study of CEO's, 80% of them were said to be optimists. That says a lot to the functioning of the company they run. Imagine the leader up on the top who is a grouch. How would everyone below them be, a bunch of grouches! Optimism is positive expectation of future events. More and more organizations are looking for answers in leaders that can handle stress with a optimistic outlook as this cascades down the ladder to the rest of the organization.

Research has shown that people who consistently read sad newspaper articles in turn look at death and disease more frequently are pessimists than people who read newspapers with pleasant news and are optimists. The results are that optimistic people make positive choices and optimistic judgment calls whereas pessimists make negative ones. As part of confident leadership you should be aware of the failures and losses of the past and study them (but in optimistic fashion) in order to avoid and improve results later, an attitude adjustment if the past was to keep yourself locked in bad news. Now you can look at adjusting and working on optimistic confident attitudes.

Cognitive dissonance

Psychologists have identified cognitive dissonance as when we behave in a way that is not natural to our consistent ways. When this happens we make every effort to get back to that normal state. This unnatural state is called cognitive dissonance and we will do anything to rid ourselves of it. An example of this is when we cross our arms (do it the way you normally would), now cross your arms the other way (you should feel a bit weird) this is cognitive dissonance. We operate in cognition and in these cognitions (thoughts) we know what our regular attitudes and behaviours are. If we do something that is outside of our everyday behaviour cognitive dissonance is happening.

"Never give an order that can't be obeyed."— General Douglas MacArthur

This is a state that many of your followers experience in the times of change, you are asking them to be different from what they are and they fight back. They are going through cognitive dissonance, they are experiencing something outside of their comfort zones and they want to rid themselves of it. You can do two things, first restore consistency to their cognition in some way or your can force your way until they agree to your terms. If you do the forcing expect much friction between you and your opponent(s).

The Red Slide

When people are in dissonance you have several things that you can do to restore consistency or in technical lingo, consonance. The first technique to is reduce the importance of the fighting thoughts. The less important the thought the more comfort that person has with it, the lighter it becomes. Second, you can keep adding more thoughts that do not conflict with the attitude. For example, buying online is easy, everybody buys on line, buying online makes you a smarter shopper, since you are a smarter shopper you save money. Lastly, the way to reduce dissonance in people is to change one of the thoughts that keep bothering, either convincing themselves or stop thinking about it.

Why is this piece important to memorize. We often are so caught up in our own goals and desires that we ignore everything else around us, causing the people around our presence to go nauseous before us. Identifying that there will be dissonance in people whether they know it or not is important so that you do not catch yourself off guard. Keep a eye on yourself as well, when things do not go our way we experience dissonance and this reflects in our attitude overall.

"There are three essentials to leadership: Humility, clarity and courage."— Fuchan Yuan

_____

AVOIDING EXTREME SELFISHNESS AND NARCISSISM

Narcissus was a Thespian hunter who was admired by all for his beauty. He was so in love with himself that when he walked by a pool he saw his reflection and could not turn away, ultimately he fell in and drowned himself. The Greeks knew the foundational elements to make a civilized society and strong leaders. Narcissism being one of the road blocks in building such a leader.

If you are fixed in your own little world, everyday living for yourself and thinking that the universe needs to bend over backwards for you, you might be a Narcissus. It is curable, this fixation of yourself and whatever it is you think you are beautiful at. Im not talking about being positive here, or giving yourself a pat on the back, that is all good. I'm talking about what the Greeks termed Narcissism, when someone is so in love with themselves that they ignore the world around them and alienating themselves and their relationships.

Narcissism plays with a person's self-respect which is easily shaken. How often do we find ourselves caught in the life of 'stuff'. I call it stuff because we are preoccupied with the little vain details that hurt relationships, our bank accounts and our future. We take things too personally, our vanity is too strong.

26

Narcissism in a group does not strengthen the group but opens vulnerabilities that group may have. Individuals are careful to open up to a narcissistic leader as they might fear they will use their position to self serve above the group members.

Narcissism is a reflection of vanity, we value our opinion too much. If you take a look and observe leaders who are successful, they are the most humble individuals you will come across. To learn something and become a master at it you need humility not narcissism and vanity.

Imagine vanity as a fortified castle, you might feel safe and secure behind the strong stone walls. Intruders cannot get to you because you are protected, you built a strong wall to ward off external threats. This however is not good. In your protected state you are actually isolating yourself from the world outside that is offering you a better life. If you stay in the castle you die.

"To command is to serve, nothing more and nothing less."—Andre Malraux

We often see movie personas with narcissist behaviours, often portraying intellectuals who condescend others around them. While a narcissistic leader can be superb in management and skill levels of leadership, his vanity will deter anyone who is following him/her. The lone point of leadership's nature is being separated from the group- this is amplified by being a narcissus.

The Red Slide

If the ancient Greeks were alive today they would have a overabundance of material to write about in regards to modern day Narcissists. Watch reality television and you will witness these behaviours, they are also emulated around you in school, work and even at home maybe even from your spouse. Modern society has brought its own undoing, by making people constantly crave attention, praise and envy from one another. We keep calling it keeping up with Joneses nowadays.

The big question is WHY?! Also why have we accepted this behaviour in our own lives?

Leadership is about collaboration and respect and humility and servant hood, all terms that modern media and critics scoff at. You will notice people in your life that love themselves, to the point they destroy their relationships, they don't listen to others, they ignore process, they are their own worst enemy. They stop learning and working for the good of others, they learn to only serve themselves.

Narcissist people often do not know that they are in love with themselves, much like our Greek character. They posses talents that others would dream of, but they are so occupied with their own being they never share these talents with anyone or the limited few. Much like Narciss who could not love anyone and left a trail of broken hearts behind him. The reality of these people is often real, they never achieve greatness and they do leave a legacy, a negative one.

The narcissist is addicted to a drug called narcissistic supply and they must have it often. It involves all forms of attention, both positive and negative. We see these people all around us, jockeying for position to get in good with the boss, always on or around a camera. Take a look at the 'selfie' phenomenon, everyone seems to be on this brainless narcissistic supply currently. The narcissist can identify, the emotional needs and hopes and fear to an almost xray vision degree to leech out the needed drug. Narcissists never regret what they do because in their eyes they are not responsible for their actions. If you have to deal with a narcissist on a daily basis it can be very daunting and exhausting.

This way of life and behaving can lead to serious consequences. In medical terms it is called narcissistic personality disorder-where these people are grouped in as having exaggerated feelings of self importance. We all have met some of these folks in our lives, the question is are you one of them? If you are the ability to lead others will be very difficult indeed.

> "Don't necessarily avoid sharp edges. Occasionally they are necessary to leadership."—Donald Rumsfeld

Here are some symptoms to look at if you fall into this:

1. You look towards others for approval and define yourself based on their standards.

2. You worry about what others say and what their reaction will be.

3. Your personal standards are unreasonably high in the pursuit of seeing yourself above others.

4. You are confused about your motivations, you lack clarity on why you do something.

5. Your relationships are superficial and serve your self esteem

6. You have a feeling of entitlement

7. You condescend others who are below your role.

8. You seek attention constantly at whatever cost.

Now, to be fair you probably found yourself in one of these characteristics. We all do from time to time. The trick is to see it and adjust and stop the infection before it spreads. The other terms used by psychologists for defining narcissism are:

1. Grandiosity

2. Arrogant and domineering

3. Preoccupation with success and getting power

4. Lack of empathy

5. Belief of being unique

6. Requiring excessive admiration

7. Sense of entitlement

8. Exploitative

9. Envious of others

For those who can control these qualities there is nothing to worry about as we can gauge these characteristics and identify when they are taking over rational actions. For those who do not know how to identify and end these, it is like a boiling pot of water that will explode-and this is a real danger. The interesting thing is that to be clinically diagnosed with NPD you need to have five of these qualities consuming you at the same time. Meaning most of us possess one of these qualities at one time or another.

Generations now are beginning to feel more and more entitled to success without putting up the efforts to achieve it. This is Narcissistic behaviour in that it changes our psychology of what we should be doing rather than what is owed to us. Nobody owes us anything, you have to work for it. Narcissism is only amplified with the absence of learning and tribulation in life. Narcissus really didn't have a difficult time in his life, he got anything he wanted, he got away with anything, but it all caught up to him. Let this be a lesson to you, love others more

"I cannot give you the formula for success, but i can give you the formula for failure, which is: Try to please everybody."— Herbert Swope

than you love yourself.

The connection that researchers are trying to discover now is between narcissism and psychopaths. It is estimated that 1 in every 200 people in Britain (and more so I other developed countries) display 5 or more of the NPD characteristics, however, majority of them are not violent or in prison. Others call narcissists ego maniacs. When the ego get too bloated and turns a person into a monster. Egomania is the layman's term for narcissistic personality disorder.

The ego maniac can be seen in these forms:

1. The over achiever. Usually drunk with success they rationalize that their arrogance is only the product of them being the best. Justifying crushing anyone that is in their way, because after all people in second place really don't know what they are doing. In their world, they claim they are the best in everything that they ever tried. Best skier-skied once, best golfer-plays a round a month, best race car driver-fastest ever driven 150km/hr and so on. Their ego's cloud their reality, and everyone is laughing except for them.

2. Cold hearted bastard. They usually don't get the big picture. The lack of empathy they exert is not even enough to fill an empty glass. It's really subtle having a lack of empathy, they just don't care. Like Narcissus they are preoccupied with themselves to care about others. Lack of

feelings for guilty actions or remorse don't exist. These cases can result in the person not having any emotional connection to their kin, at a funeral of their relatives they probably wouldn't shed a tear.

3. Boss the egomaniac. Ego's do not pick gender, they can just as easily be female. Charming, personable and friendly are the introductory qualities to open people up to them like a can of sardines. They often give the employees the delusion that their relationship will be collaborative. Often over time the behaviour changes rapidly and criticism sets in with a cool type of attitude. Often unexpected they announce that "we are watching you", "we are monitoring your performance." Without you knowing about it, what it is about, and how long has it been going on. Most narcissists become bullies in the workplace. Taunting, torturing and sadistically inflicting pain (most often emotional) unnecessarily. They are obsequious to their superiors but to their followers they are sadists. These bosses resent weakness and weak people, or even appearing weak they will make you their target. They have an inbred aversion to the elderly, children and sick people. Anyone that they cannot use they wont hang around. This provokes in the narcissistic boss a sadistic impulse to eliminate them from their sphere of influence instead of help them out. The narcissist boss is a predator.

4. The cult leader. This is the extreme case of a narcissist and it involves seven or more of the clinical disorders, most emphasis given on admiration and exploitation of others. Religion is a perfect tool for a narcissist to control others. NPD's are made for cult leadership in that religion is a tailor made program for their sadistic fantasies. What better way to express yourself than to be like God. Often times these individuals claim that they are the only ones who can deliver the message from God and that their words are the words of God. They are the messengers of a divine being and the cult is to do their 'action'.

5. The psychopath. This most rare of individuals displays all nine traits and is very hard to find or spot. Usually very intelligent they find ways to get what they want. Never hint that a narcissist is ignorant, or incapable or weak, never criticize, never disagree with a narcissist or you could trigger a reaction of epic proportions.

6. The self aware narcissist. Most narcissist do not have the ability to step on the sidelines and look at themselves from a different point of view. They are too self absorbed. Being aware, however, does not help. Taking a heroin addict and knowing they are aware of their addiction does not make them stop using the drug. They cannot work in teams, they cannot hold a job, they cannot sustain any social interaction with

the outside world. They are consumed by themselves. It is ironic. They want to be in absolute control of everything, hence their awareness of their condition, the self aware narcissist contains the 9 traits and they are aware of the poison but cannot fix their mental state. Because they need to be in control all the time, their challenge to authority proves unsuccessful most of the time, causing much anger and rage.

It is very difficult to cure a personality disorder as it is a stable and long time developing process. It is part of their consciousness and being. And your attempt to change that in a narcissist, especially one with five or more traits can prove troublesome. Your realization of a narcissist in your midst needs to be of observation of the traits that make them up and their personality. If you sense that it exists on a constant level within you teams and followers address it with professional help.

The understanding that you gain from controlling these qualities will prove useful to your leadership skills. It is very difficult to find the attitude 'I'm the best at my job' as a condition which should be treated, and accusing anyone of NPD would not be wise. What is certain is that the shift in mentality in society and how new generations are being raised is that the qualities are being amplified each new generation. A concerning threat to the actual productivity of a society, not just boasting or all puff and no filler type of society.

" Whoever loves becomes humble. Those who love have, so to speak, pawned a part of their narcissism."

Sigmund Freud

BUILDING STRENGTH THROUGH EMPOWERMENT

Who dares wins:
"We are the pilgrims, master; we shall go
Always a little further: it may be
Beyond that last blue mountain barred with snow
Across that angry or that glimmering sea..."

James Elroy Flecker- The Golden Road to Samarkand

(inscribed on the regimental clock tower at Stirling Lines-SAS members who 'failed to beat the clock')

What are people thinking? Is the question you should be asking yourself almost on a daily basis. As a leader of a group, whether small or large or even for your business you should be aware of what is going on in the heads of your followers.

The reality is that most people think about themselves most of the time. We are so distracted with what is going on with us that we rarely step out of this skull prison to think about what others might be doing. The right way to start empowering others is to put yourself in their shoes. Try to imagine what is going on in their heads, if you cant come up with some answers then don't expect your empowering to work.

Empowerment involves several pieces to work. The first piece is in yourself, you cannot be motivated by your own selfish desires, getting results, or timelines are up etc. Empowering, also known as motivating, encouraging, enchanting is about getting the other person to feel the benefits as well. Before we dive into the details here is when you should not empower people.

"Leaders must be close enough to relate to others, but far enough ahead to motivate them."—John C. Maxwell

1. Are you asking people to do something that you yourself wouldn't do? If the answer is yes, then stop. It is not worth your integrity and your reputation. This is manipulation and this technique once found out hurts you in the long run.

2. Find out if your interests are conflicting? The way empowerment works is if both parties are aligned, this is also a ethical debate. If they do not align, then reconsider your proposal or revisit the target audience.

3. Are you concealing anything from your people? Lets say that your interests are in line. Should you disclose other information. If the information is necessary for the results to happen, then yes you should.

4. Are you using 'white lies'? Sometimes people don't need to know everything right? Wrong.

Again this is interpreted as manipulation and once found out your trust with your followers will be diminished to 0. Anything you truthfully do in the future will be taken as a lie.

5. Are you empowering people who are easy targets? The gullible are easily swayed, or the hurt, or people who are facing a crisis in their lives. This is immoral to do. Success is not built on the backs of the meek. This doesn't help you either, you will psyche yourself into thinking that your skills are good, while in reality they suck.

If your answer to the above questions was a yes then you need to reconsider leadership of any kind. You could fool a couple of people but you will be found out and the fall will be great. Turn away from the dark side and reshape your life.

Empowerment is tricky, even good leaders that have been around for quite some time find themselves questioning why they empowered someone. I have a example, let's call this manager Jimmy. I promoted Jimmy to a high management position only to hear that Jimmy was talking behind my back. When I found out Jimmy had long moved on, Jimmy lost the big picture and could not see that without a leaders empowerment he probably would not have been where he was. Shame on me for believing Jimmy was a stand up guy. The only thing you can do when something like this happens to you is to move on, Jimmy will be found out soon enough. Empowerment is more than just motivation, it means that you are doing your job as a leader and holding yourself accountable for the well being of your team.

Empowerment Toolbox

How do companies keep producing more results while lowering their resources? The result of productivity is a measurement of empowerment of the workers. As a leader you need to get a high ROI or rather the ROE (return on energy).

The issue with many companies is that unclear communication and direction from direct supervisors on what employees are supposed to be doing results in about 50% of wasted time at work. People gossip, water cooler talk, avoid deadlines basically are there to do as little as possible because of the unorganized and unmotivated nature of their managers. Leaders see this gap and address it by empowerment. They propose a shift in attitude.

"Our chief want is someone who will inspire us to be what we know we could be." — Ralph Waldo Emerson

Your ability to communicate your message to your teams and have them become self sufficient while building new skills is the goal of empowerment. Your time that you have is not enough to cover all the bases, what your goal should be is, to collectively empower your employees to be autonomous. As Napoleon said "there are no bad soldiers under a good general.", your ability to train and keep motivated your "soldiers" will free up a lot of time on your end.

I often get managers coming to me saying that they did not have the time to finish tasks xyz. The reason they didn't finish everything is because they were doing it themselves not their people, rather the inability to build relationships. Their powerlessness to convince the group to work together or to work on a given task in a timely manner is their faults as a leader who cannot empower. You might have managers, or kids that you are struggling with. Your ability to empower them will depend on if you follow the following:

1. Do not lecture or display superiority.

2. Avoid criticism and show respect for your people.

3. Let people fail.

4. Hold people accountable.

If you notice that I did not mention anything about KPI's or how to plot a matrix of whatever and who knows what. These qualities are not based on the people you are trying to change, they are based on you. Your self-image and experience will determine for the large part on, if your employees and managers want to be empowered. Do they feel the respect from you and do you have their backs if they make a mistake.

"Victory has a hundred fathers and defeat is a orphan."— John F. Kennedy

They have to know that you believe in them. End of story.

Humans are for the most part 100% emotional beings. They first decide on decisions emotionally and then look at things rationally. In that order. Emotional decisions are made immediately. The fight or flight response is part of the human condition and its charged by emotional experiences. If a person you are trying to empower or motivate is used to getting criticism from you and negativity then they will be hard to move. Psychology names, negativity as a bad feeling that humans lose control over.

In thinking about relationships we can look at Aristotle's Nicomachean Ethics. Which explains the motivation behind human interaction and action- is happiness. The action that humans beings take on certain goals in life lies a hidden unwritten often unrealized goal, which is "are we happy with what we are doing?". Aristotle's book distinguished three ways that people look at happiness:

1. Pleasure in all areas of life

2. Honour in life, the path to wisdom

3. Contemplation

These common pieces of happiness are what your managers and employees are seeking in one form or another and are key to empowerment. Even if they are not aware of the underlying motivation for their goals they are still seeking some form of happiness in their lives. Understanding this will ultimately make your job as their leader that much more effective.

Your ability to empower is rooted in the desires of your employee's happiness. Why do they work for you? Why do they listen? There seems to be motivators like, money, promotions, acceptance etc. However, the reality is that they seek happiness from anywhere, and if you can provide them this they will listen to you and your message.

Knowing that happiness is important to your employees and using the three characteristics above of what not to do, because that would impede their happiness, you need to explain the why to your people. Why is it we are doing this?

My first management job involved a retail location that was falling apart both operationally and structurally. When I started asking why we are in business, out of the 110 employees including the management team, nobody knew why we were there. A sad existence to be in. To be coming to work to collect a paycheque is the way most people are living nowadays. Given them a purpose to be there, a collective group that knows the why, they will have the energy to solve most of your organizations problems.

The three wise men: Aristotle, Plato and Socrates

You might wonder what the hell these three ancient philosophers have to do with leadership, let alone empowerment and engagement. It all started when someone started to ask the question why, and throw away dogma and divine intervention as the answer to everything. Critical thought leaders, these philosophers of three are the foundations of which much of our society is based on today. Their reflections and research are the truths of human nature, and when you understand human thought you can identify what is missing to motivate it.

To the ancient mathematicians and philosophers, they believed and knew that there were rules for everything. Anything could be expressed in a mathematical or scientific process. Music for instance, guitars have ratios that are equivalent to the length of the string being plucked, a discovery that was made by Pythagoras (often said to be one of the most important people that ever lived).

"He who cannot be a good follower cannot be a good leader."— Aristotle

Close observation from men like Pythagoras made the ancient world more bearable and launched changes into society that propelled their prosperity over others. Asclepius was the greek god of healing and medicine, however, the Greeks did not stop at their gods. They made advances into the healing powers of the mind, and the Asclepians (Greeks who lived in that region) were famous for their psychoanalytic methods and activities. A visit to Epidaurus was one similar to us going to a shrink. In Epidaurus was a theatre where acting and living out your emotions was considered a healing process to vent.

The Red Slide

To illustrate the power the Greeks had in thought and innovation, imagine yourself a non-greek looking in. The way they carried themselves, the things they talked about, how they dressed and a conducted themselves. They were almost alien like. A totally superior species of human, made possible by the concentrated efforts of a few thought leaders. Driven by a few who knew how to organize and empower.

Why are these men important we will get into in just a minute. We should understand the building blocks from where this civilization came from and where it went, becoming a symbol of advancement and civility for the modern world.

Laws make things predictable, and as such they need to be used in order to save time. Leadership also has many laws. In regards to empowering and motivating there are numerous psychological laws that need to be followed.

Socrates made his claims by observing people. The shoemaker should have the skills to make shoes, the politician should have the skills to do politics, and the leader should have the skills to lead. Like Socrates, you observe your team, if they are specialized they need to have the skills to do their craft. The motivating factor comes into play when their leader, you, identify that they are missing skills and you offer to provide training and help, you find the tools and experts who will train them. Socrates sought to understand how we should live, not what the "Gods" were telling us through mystics and signs of nature. The Athenian lifestyle made him understand that men are foolish and even the good man can do foolish things without being aware. The cultivation of the soul, what Socrates called the progress of living well and practicing this life is what a leader does to cultivate his skills and learning. In motivation the essence is to understand and observe not to enforce. Ineffective motivators use force or sadistic ways to get their people going, while this works, it is a short term strategy. Socrates believed that the fundamental point of human life is to seek the meaning of questions, seek answers to keep looking. It is not what you find but the journey to finding. Great leaders did not become great by chance, the many failures they had were not recorded making them more grandiose than they really are; however they never stopped looking.

"Being responsible sometimes means pissing people off."—Colin Powell

Socrates also taught that we should be leaving the material pleasures of the world and focus on our souls. What this correlates into a leadership life and in regards to motivating people is that leaders should lead because it is their calling to raise people from the ashes into success not because of the paycheque that is involved. Materialistic wants in leadership cloud the judgment and energy, because what happens when we achieve our materialistic goal, we deflate and feel empty. Leadership and motivation involve a spiritual and psychological element that is hard to define. That is why many leaders are ineffective in motivation; they focus too much on what they will "get" from motivating and not what their followers will "receive".

Socrates is important to us for leadership as he emphasized argument or dialect, or debate if you will. The motivating characteristic if we connect it to true motivations of people is, why are we doing this. If this answer cannot be argued then motivation is stale and unreal. Arguing actually solidifies the group and their motivation to complete a task. Debate and argument should be facilitated by you the leader, but everyone should express as much as possible their thoughts and challenge the idea. This is a moral standpoint for leaders, as corruption is the absence of argument and totalitarian power, killing motivation and empowerment. Asking questions where there are questions to be asked, not taking things for what they seem but observing and challenging, not remaining content-this is the Socratic way of thinking.

Plato, was a student of Socrates. Socrates was his greatest influence. Plato believed that people were ready to accept things right at their face value. As a leader, in a leadership role you should be wary of how people seem to be "motivated" and if this is true and long lasting. Believing that people bought into your speech or process is not a smart strategy as many chameleons and yes men/women exist. Looking to further advance their personal interest they will agree and pretend to everything you say. Plato believed that good was absolute, and reality is that all of us want to live well-whatever that means to each of us. Some do this to get you off their scent and scheme while you have the best intensions for them. Ignoring them is the best way to combat their behaviour.

Aristotle joined Plato's academy when he was 18 and stayed for 20 years. Very possibly his most talked about work the ten predicates can be correlated to motivation and empowerment in some way. They are:

1. **Substance**: Understanding what Aristotle wanted to say of substance might take some time. When we mention substance it involves particular subjects. For example, we might say "I need to motivate that person", you are not motivating his image or how they look, or their hair style or their car or possessions, you are motivating them, their essence of humanity. You say to yourself "I need to motivate Johnny", you are referring to his substance and nothing else of him.

2. **Quantity**: There are two parts discrete or continuous. What we will interpret for leadership is does motivation need to be a one time deal or do you need to constantly keep up. If it is a long project that is daunting with a lot of new people, a continuous approach might work.

3. **Quality**: This emphasizes the nature of motivation that is required. Speech, body language, dress, tone, male, female, capability etc. Learning what you audience needs helps

you identify which areas you need to raise to a new level.

4. **Relation**: Is who you are trying to empower related to anyone or anything else. If there is more than one person who is trying to be empowered they are related in Aristotle's eyes. Leadership needs to know the depth of connectors that are involved in engagement. Many employees talk to each other and they share stories or management and the company, they will share ideas that are presented to them, this is their relation.

5. **Place**: Where will you do you motivating and empowering. At the water cooler? Maybe. Do you do it in a theatre or in a formal setting? This is the actual physical place where you would motivate your people, pick it wisely, a bad place and they might get distracted or feel disrespected by your choice of environment.

6. **When**: Do you try to motivate people when its time to go home, or after lunch? Motivating or trying to empower people after defeat is not good also, nobody want to keep trudging in second place. Plan on motivation and empowerment well before

"And if the blind lead the blind, both shall fall into the ditch."—Bible

the bridges are

burned so people know that they have some time to make these things happen.

7. **Posture, Attitude, Position**: When you speak to your follower and team members how to they listen to you, standing up? Lying down, sitting? Slouched across the table. The importance of this state is that the connection between a standing and sitting motivational absorption is drastic. While standing people pay attention more, if you can do this the better your message will get across.

8. **Having**: Wise generals know that to keep their soldiers motivated they keep their bellies full. If you team is suffering from some materialistic problem (personal or company associated) you need to understand this and adjust your method. It's hard to get motivated if you are going through a divorce, or a bankruptcy. Ask yourself if you can help out, if you can perfect, on the other hand if the tools are company associated and they need them to keep going you should fight for those.

9. **Action**: In your actual empowering and motivating are you prepared, do you know what to say and are you saying it the way you imagined it. Nothing is worse than a smart leader who cannot display what they need to the group. It makes them look silly and foolish.

10. **Being affected**: Aristotle defined this as a state of suffering or undergoing some state. While in motivation mode, do your words and ideas make people uncomfortable and uneasy? Are these ideologies in your empowerment that are debatable to everyone else except for you. We can look at leaders such as Stalin and Hitler and see that while their motivation to their people was effective their overall result were catastrophic for the rest of the world.

Aristotle's main belief was that happiness was an activity not a state or disposition. It is the "me", in his philosophy of men that he defines our nature. The man who fears and avoids everything and has not the ability to stand up to anything transforms into a coward. The man who is afraid of nothing at all and rushes into danger is foolish. The leader who does not know his people but want to lead is going to fail.

Motivating different generations

You have baby boomers, millenials, gen-x and soon gen z. How do you get all this time line to listen to your lead? We should look at the different generations as they play a role into your decision making for empowerment and planning. Knowing who is who and what ticks them off will save you time if not energy.

Baby boomers: The current trend for baby boomers is that they like to keep working. Even more, they want to keep working past their retirement age, even in different fields as part time work. These folks grew up on sweat and the motto "the only helping hand you're gonna get is at the end of your elbow." . Baby boomers have changed the face of society in all aspects, from education, engineering, finance and most of all leadership. So if they are going into retirement why are they so important to your leadership quest? The answer is that they hold all the wisdom from their experiences and mistakes so that current generations do not have to repeat them. They are a tricky bunch though. They need to be cajoled into giving you the answers. They necessarily do not need motivation to get something done, its in their DNA to get stuff done its who they are. They, however, want respect-bottom line. They want to know that the people who are going to use their knowledge and expertise are worthy of that intellect and invested time. Their generation experienced almost all of the drastic changes in our society over the last 60 -70 years, they are a gold mine of information if you know how to approach them.

This generation is usually the wisest in the room, however, not the most confrontational or loudest, which often makes them unnoticeable. They usually are laughing at the silly ideas most younger generations are spitting out, instead of stepping on the ball and figuring it out once and calling out mistakes before they are actioned.

Baby boomers do not like to repeat things, they believe in measuring twice and cutting once. If millennial's are playing pac man, baby boomers are playing chess. They strategize instead of going head first through issues. Their prime years were defined by economic turmoil and world unrest. While younger generations will not experience (lets hope) world wars and global nuclear crisis, baby boomers were defined by it. This makes them very centred and realistic in expectations as leaders and as leader supporters.

The motivation(s) behind this group are that they want to transfuse their knowledge into the next generation, that is their goal. They have just spent the last 40 or 50 years working, the thought that much of what they learned will be wasted is unbearable to baby boomers. To give this knowledge to anyone is also out of the question, it must be earned. Imagine it like the apprentice going to the Shaolin temple to be trained by the grand master, you must earn the masters trust in order to learn their secrets, often doing trivial and senseless things. Baby boomers like to test younger generation as well as young leaders, after all, they've had their share of leaders in their lives, what's another on the list. If you do prove your worth then the will spill out their wisdom to you and the 'worthy' like a dam.

> "There has never been a meaningful life built on easy street."—John Paul Warren

Currently in Canada the percentage of Baby boomers that encompass the population is about 32% which is the highest percentage of any generation. In other words 1/3 of your group that you will be leading in the next ten years, and maybe more will be a baby boomer. Understanding this generation will determine your success. Depending on what kind of organization you work for or are leading assume that not everyone

53

is motivated by the same things. Baby boomers have a unique outlook on life and what is going on around them, utilize them as much as you can.

Generation X: The average house in 1965 was $13,000 USD and the average income per year was $6,450 USD. Malcolm X gets shot in New York. Jk Rowling is born on July 31st and 35,000 people march on Washington to protest the Vietnam war.

This generation is defined by changes in time and the moulding of a tough transition to modernization and economic acceleration. If anyone is used to change it's this generation, they've known nothing else but change and their intellectual horsepower is your winning ticket. Anyone who has worked with a Gen x now, around 35-50 years old knows that they are in charge. They know what they are doing and know how to get it. Majority of our modern billionaires fall into this early generation category. They are the product of a time where there wasn't time to think about our feelings about things, they needed to do and get on with life. The global environment made sure of it that they got both the education and experience to lead future generations. The technological changes experience in their early childhood influenced many to go into the fields of technology and make their mark there while others were fighting the economy with their business ideas.

This generation has a rich influence on what the decisions should be when in a group setting. They are the current leaders of much of what we do now. They are influenced by technology and the good it brings, mostly associated with their childhood fascination with the changes that happened in the 1980's.

This generation might not get along with baby boomers, much of what they did was develop values of their own, not what the baby boomers wanted them to do, their parents. Rebelling against the 1960's and blazing a trail for themselves. This generation is quite stubborn and head strong. They often do not back down from a fight.

"Surround yourself with great people; delegate authority; get out of the way."—Ronald

I had a Gen x manager who in her defence was a valuable member to a certain point. Her inability to follow direction made her difficult to work with, because she thought her way was better than what the management team came to agree upon, this ended up costing her job. This gen x populace is known for trying out risky things because they will not be told what they can and can't do, by anyone, including you.

When motivating these individuals you need to keep in mind that many of them were affected by the recession more severely than the other generations. In their 30's they should have had real income growth instead many lost their jobs, their savings and racked up debt in the process. Their capability is clear and sound, their issue is trust. Can they trust you to lead them in the right direction? You will have to display and show the numbers before they jump on your ship soon.

Generation X is risk averse. They think before they leap, being in a time when good jobs are hard to come by and the ever increasing competition it is a rule rather than attitude. Your job is to convince the performers to take a chance at moving ahead, with their knowledge you can get the job done, because they know how, but they are often caught in their own mental force field that embeds them sometimes to inaction.

Generation X'ers account for about 84 million people in the U.S. in 2011. Much of them look at leadership through a skeptics glasses. They really need to be convinced that you are their leader, through authenticity not fluff.

Millenials: This generation compared to the others is the hardest to control and satisfy. It can be summarized in three words.

ME, ME, ME.

They have been characterized as complaining excessively about entitlement and often have a touch of narcissism. They are, however, large optimists of the future. The right leader who can show them the way will win their votes. Your goal is to include them as much as possible in the planning pieces of your work and teams. They always see the bright side of something new, on how it can work, they have vast imaginations.

Generation Y or Millenials have been influenced by the e-age. They grew up on instant information and gratification. Their diverse knowledge base often hurts them more than it helps as they are jack of all trades and master's of none. The restlessness that you encounter with this generation is a result of their interaction with the e-world. Their communications are largely based on texts, Skype and email, not to mention Facebook and other social media outlets. Which says that they are time sensitive.

This behaviour displays the narcissistic pieces of a millennial, where they always need to have their phones with them, god forbid that they miss a text reply within 5 minutes. Observe around yourself a bit and you'll see the infectious nature of the technology that many of them cannot do without.

"Cream always rises to the top...so do good leaders."—John Paul Warren

Your approach to leading this group needs to be a consensus based approach. They themselves need to agree on the solution or path, only when they cannot reach a solution do they relinquish power and give you the choice to pick for them. You could do it your way, and bully your way through a decision, however you will see that progress will be very, very slow.

Some authors refer to this generation as trophy kids. Where in their life just participating in something makes you a winner. It is unfortunate that our culture in America is producing weaker citizens while other countries are enforcing strict discipline to excellence. Enlightened yet ineffective.

It is not the millenials fault they are like this, well not entirely. Many millenials are still underemployed or unemployed with the depression reeking havoc on the global economy even today in 2015. Many of them still with their parents. It seems that this could have long term effects on their motivation to succeed as there is no end in sight.

This is a even more challenging thought when your leadership is questioned with this generation. Why should they invest their time in you? Their world is at a standstill and they need answers. You will supply them with the answers, the first one is on me, it's called get off your butt to work and work hard.

Leaders should question hard, in the next 10 years when the majority of the workforce will be millenials, how they will need to be lead. What will motivate and engage this generation to work harder and repair previous debacles of society. Leaders need to think about this now before the millennial generation goes too far off.

SELF DISCOVERY WITH EMOTIONAL INTELLIGENCE

If you are the bus driver and want to go somewhere important, you want to make sure that you get the right people on the bus and the wrong people off. To do this you must manage your emotions and know when to react and when to hold back. Everyone has bad days, but if you have high EQ you will know when to bite your tongue when a bad day comes around.

The difficulty in this situation as the leader is to identify who is right and gets to stay and who is go get off. You ability to measure others is based on your emotional intelligence. Physiologists who study this, associate emotions with the bodily interactions of the environment, up to including hormonal activity, circulation of the blood, respiration, body temperature and gastrointestinal activity. These conditions, in whatever state they happen to be in influence your emotions, which in turn influence your reactions and responses.

> "The ruler attains wholeness in the correct governance of the people."— Lao Tzu

People with good EQ are able to know the feelings that they are going through.

While we have been using this skill for a very long time emotional intelligence has been introduced to us just recently and has been the use of many leaders and managers trying to improve their performance and their teams. It is still clear that many are avoiding EQ and its uses or are just ignorant to how to use it.

The arousal of emotions is connected to the way we perceive our current situation (by the use of our Amygdala), these arousals are magnified if the situation is unclear or new to us. Humans compare the state they are in now, with similar experiences of the past, where the stimulation of this new state (the new experience) often exceeds the threshold of what they are used to, thus the arousal of a new emotional state. When we observe people in a new environment they are held back or extremely friendly, two sides that operate on either end of EQ. There is little stability when experiencing something new. They experience cognitive dissonance.

Empirical data, has proven this in the common emotions such as sadness, happiness, fear, love, hate, disgust and sexual desire in the above mentioned observations. We also experience many emotional states that are connected with our 'mirror neurone' where the imitation or observation of other people's emotions affect our own. An example of this is in Chimpanzee experimentation where one chimp looks at the other chimp who is eating, the first chimp's mirror neurone fire in the same order as the one who is eating. So it is true when we see angry people, or watch television, we are influenced by sadness when we watch sad people. It is no wonder the crime rate has risen, as the influential ages of 7-16 year olds watching violence on television influences them in the same way Chimps influence each other.

Emotional intelligence is categorized in knowledge and leadership by influence. To be emotionally intelligent you should have a degree of rationality within your head. You cannot be emotionally intelligent and savvy if you are a explosive person who reacts to situations-explaining irrational behaviour. There are successful people in our time who are not emotionally intelligent, it is evident in their behaviour with others-sports figures, such as Dennis Rodman for his antics and 'freedom of speech' could be said that he is intelligent and successful but not emotionally intelligent as self -centred and egotistical are not included in EQ.

"Sheep are always looking for a new shepherd when the terrain gets rocky."—Karen Marie Moning

There are several reasons you should practice emotional intelligence on a daily basis. First, your ability to control your emotions helps you learn new skills faster and absorb new ideas. If you suffer from anxiety and fear, these emotions impede you ability to absorb outside information as you are too consumed with your perceptions. Humans have a hard time learning and adjusting their learning strategy in strenuous and stressful situations because of improper functioning of neuronal and hormonal conditions.

Second, EQ adjusts your perceptions which are influenced by emotions and various emotional states. The two levels that we need to perceive are sensory and interpretations. The sensory level is instinctual and reactive, interpretive includes our experiences. The emotional disturbance that we encounter is caused by current perceptions interacting with emotional states. Low EQ people are constantly afraid because they programmed themselves to be that way in states of change around them. Notice around you the successful colleagues that seem to always get what they want, look at their attitude and you'll know why. Their perception is not altered by fear of the unknown.

Emotions have several components and are connected to the psychological state of the individual. Researchers have defined these components into three categories: cognitive, evaluation, and motivation.

1. Cognitive component:

This part gives the user the information that is necessary to process the situation. People who are new at a job and have little experience will have a hard time understanding and get frustrated easily on the job. It is your job to understand where they stand. You should stay patient and they should be open minded.

"I am more afraid of an army of 100 sheep lead by a lion, than an army of 100 lions led by a sheep."— Talleyrand

2. Evaluation component:

Hateful emotions negatively evaluate people and their perception of the situation. Pride overestimates a person's ability to do something. Regret is the result of wrong commitments in what the person wanted to do. Again if we assess the emotional states we go through and ask ourselves in this evaluation phase you become the guru leader. You would be able to identify from peoples actions what state they are going through by using and understanding the evaluation component.

3. Motivation component:

Psychologists exist to fix many motivational components in people. The desire or willingness to stay at a emotional state depends on this component. Blatant behaviour of individuals can be associated with motivational states of what they are trying to achieve. Sometimes a overly angry person is trying to get attention from someone.

The question for you as the leader should be, how much should I invest of my time to build EQ? Does it really matter in the end, does performance of my company increase if my EQ and my teams EQ's are raised.

Lets take a look at a car dealership. There are two salespeople that you meet. One is a low performer and the other is a high performer. Both have similar training in sales and both have similar educational backgrounds. The high performer however, I able to identify his audience and clients and is able to adjust his behaviour to that particular buyer. The low performer keeps doing what he wants and what he thinks is right. You get the picture?

We have these people in our spheres of influence as well. The whole world and every business in the world has this example in one form or another. Some people are successful more than others because they know how to read the 'temperature' of the room and adjust to it. Since you are part of the room you should also read your own temperature and adjust.

The ability to think of what it is that you are experiencing is called meta-cognition and it is very useful in identifying what to do next. Both for yourself and your followers. Have you ever caught yourself stopping in the middle of a thought and asking yourself what you are doing? This is meta cognition and it is developed through your EQ.

Part of cognition of leadership, specifically, your leadership needs to be in the understanding of why you do things that you do. Like the old saying goes, "if you don't learn from history you are bound to repeat it.". You should be aware of your consciousness and why you do things and react the way you do. Understanding your limitations and boundaries, your faults and strengths. This paradigm shift is another way of saying that you should absorb the times you are in and flex to their ideas or be swallowed up in them.

"FOCUS=Follow On Course Until Successful."— Ifeanyi Enoch Onuoha

64

Your true leadership is in testing of yourself and how well you do against your own standards. These standards are built over time, and can be changed. They are, however, more easily identified and adjusted if self-awareness of the leader is strong, a EQ quality.

To understand your way of thinking you need to know why it is so difficult to change your way of thinking. It involves EQ but lets look at it a little more deeply.

In real life situations a change in thinking means work, (whether you are new or seasoned at your current role), the reality is that change is overwhelming and seems that way to most people. Whenever there is a shift/change in ideas the feeling of loss and control takes over their lives. A loss of control can mean someone at work made a 'smart-ass' comment about something that you weren't aware of, (people talking behind your back, that you were oblivious to) and this can throw you off your game and adjust the way you behave around people, influencing your leadership decisions. A corruption of bias.

If you have developed a set of core values early in your leadership development, change is not that hard to deal with, you values stay the same but your leadership adjusts. Your priorities are part of the whole process, and simple change that happens was already planned for in advance. Your tolerance for mistakes is high and you consciously assess others in their tolerance for these same mistakes. You do take notes on those that do not change and are not putting forth the effort to change. You hold them accountable.

You must know how to make others take charge and develop their EQ. To break free of their influences You give your group small decisions to make, often trivial to see how they will do. If they succeed proceed with bigger decisions. If they fail then it is a learning opportunity for you. Starting small in the face of changes gives you the benefit of recovering quickly.

When your EQ gets into action you know when and how to deal with many problems at hand.

Life is about not knowing, having to change, taking the moment and making the best of it, without knowing whats going to happen next. Delicious ambiguity.

-Gilda Radner-

Self-knowledge-a outcome of EQ

A leaders knowledge of him/herself is the most important skill they can possess and work on. You cannot lead unless you follow, you cannot change unless you know what change does to you.

As the stoic Marcus Aurelius wrote, we all love ourselves more than other people, however, we value their opinions more than we value our own. Do not lose faith in yourself, or what you are trying to achieve. EQ is about doubt and knowing that it exists, not the affirmation that everything is going to be ok, its not. Work on your strategy to improve yourself first, then get on with others.

Avoid telling yourself that you have it hard and that you need to get away from it all. Going on a vacation, to the country, the beach, shopping whatever you do to calm yourself is self defeating. What you need to do is dig deep within your-'self', that is the most secure and peaceful place in your life and always will be-no interruptions, no interference. Self regulation gives results.

> "Patience is a virtue not a vice."— Jaachynma N.E. Agu

Managing yourself is not about running towards a goal or gaining popularity (those are the side effects) , knowing your weaknesses and strengths is what is important. Only EQ can do that for you. No amount of counselling and training courses can 'teach' you what emotional intelligence should look like, you have to experience it through life. This is why leadership is hard, easy to read about hard to implement. We repeatedly hear from people that they do not want to be leaders, it's because it is a hard gig to do, but well worth it.

Many leaders have the goal to try and please everyone, you goal should be to- appease to most, asking yourself is what you are doing the right thing. A leader with a broken moral compass will try to please everyone, even the followers who are wolves disguised as sheep in your flock. In trying to please everyone you will not be able to identify the wolves from the sheep, you end up working harder than you have to, instead of observing a bit more.

The Red Slide

In a study of college students, researchers tested the hypothesis if emotional intelligence would have a positive effect on their lives and how the interaction of stress and EQ would affect their lives in college. While being a very subjective study, as different opinions of satisfaction are present, they found that individuals who scored high on interpersonal qualities (verbal communication, listening, negotiation, decision making etc) scored higher in life satisfaction than those who did not. The study went further and stated that individuals who scored less in their EQ had more life satisfaction. Ignorance is bliss, nobody said leading would be easy. It is important to know as a leader (but not abuse the perception) that many of the people you are leading will be low on the EQ meter.

This might be shocking for some of you, but do you remember that one person in your life that you look at and wonder how they can live with themselves, not having a care in the world. This ignorance of the outside world is not the goal what you are trying to achieve or duplicate in people. Fight the urge to give in to low EQ and live a life of ignorance, the less we know the less stress, we like to comfort ourselves.

We live in a world of massive stressors. Stress at work, stress from family, stress from the weather, financial stress –everything is out to grab you in one form or another. It would make sense to be ignorant if we live in a world such as this, and it doesn't seem to be slowing down. Many people give up and let themselves be taken by the world-what a dull life to live. The fact that you are reading this book tells me that you don't give in.

Develop emotional signals that will help you target stressors in your life and maneuver around them easier. React or respond, EQ needs to be a everyday practice that will arm you against the ignorance that wants to claw its way back into your life.

Confucius: China's greatest leadership teacher (EQ journey)

His road to wisdom and knowing was filled with failure and hardship. He simply did not want to submit to the political order he was born into, he wanted and needed to transform it. Abandoning his wife and kids, he set out to change China. He did it with peace and understanding, in other words his Emotional intelligence had to make massive changes in the way people thought in ancient China.

His incredible curiosity for learning as a child, was what probably saved him from the years of poverty that him and his mother experienced. This part of Confucius would later prove as one of his primary dogmas for the people he influenced. Being relentless in the improvement of his character Confucius shows us that emotional intelligence is self driven not externally influenced. To enhance EQ you need to be brutal with yourself and the reality that you live in.

He would later say that noble deeds not noble birth gave man honour. This is an echo for your mission in leadership as noble deeds of leading your followers and team members into areas that seem difficult is the primary objective of a highly intelligent leader, not because the position was given to you to abuse but to enhance others around you.

In the mind of Confucius, he believed that people became better the more they were educated. For leading, knowledge is in the same building. Leadership is amplified when more people know about how their emotional intelligence associates with the group. Having a whole team function perfectly, but having one person oblivious drags the whole team down. Becoming educated is a choice, a life long choice that brings fruit for years to come. As in leadership, the emotional intelligence muscles that you exercise consciously on a daily basis will serve you better for much more difficult situations that will arise in leading.

As a trick, the enemies of the young emperor who Confucius was advising, sent him three beautiful girls to distract him from the reforms that Confucius was enacting. Humiliated and humbled, he left the land in search for a way to spread his wisdom and end suffering in China. He never found the supporters in his time, however, Confucianism is making many Asian countries very prosperous who believe that the human being can make something out of himself if they work diligently at it.

As a litmus test to testing your emotional intelligence start asking people, preferably your kids first, Since they cant punch you that hard some question and comments can be tested on them. Ask them, "I need you to focus", "pay attention (with the hand gesture of two fingers from their eyes to yours)", "I need you to stay calm". Try this test and see what happens.

Now those strategies very often don't work. Why? Do you remember the reactions that you got? You might be misreading what they are experiencing and insulting them by asking those things. You assume that your emotional state is the same as theirs.

Emotional intelligence is about reading yourself as much as others. How many of us want to go for coffee with that guy who is always agitated at work. Negativity affects surrounding emotions negatively. Knowing some rules will help you prepare your interactions with people.

Rules of EQ:

1.

There are some unwritten rules that involve Emotional intelligence. Some subtle and others not so much. One of these rules is the actual location you are in, the mannerisms, the culture, the history all of these characteristics will determine how people express themselves emotionally. I come from a very open, straight to the point culture, where speaking your mind is actually natural and expected. While if I used this strategy in an Asian country such as Japan or Korea people would deem this unacceptable and disrespectful.

2.

Acknowledge that there will be "dream stealers" in your life. This rule involves a simple premise, that others people will try to steal the positivity that you own away from you. Think about this the next time someone comments, "oh so you get to go home at 4pm, you should come work where I work..." they suck the positive emotions out of you and you start questioning yourself and your lifestyle. These emotional terrorists cannot regulate themselves and use passive aggressive methods to influence others to join their misery.

3.

Avoid asking people about their emotional intelligence which is subjective and does not have validity. The reason is that everyone will say they are more emotionally intelligent and more intelligent than the other person. Nobody wants to be classified as dumb in any sense. The rule is don't question, but teach and inform about emotional intelligence. Leaders need to understand that questioning or inquiry about a followers EQ could spell disaster, making them uncomfortable with their boss or peers.

> "...emotional intelligence accounts for 80 percent of career success."— Daniel Goleman

4.

You emotional life will interfere with your cognitive life. Many students cannot take tests well if they are experiencing some life altering moment. The interference from their emotions is too great fueled by the subconscious which deters any kind of focusing ability. The same goes for in the work place. A member of your team might be going through a divorce, and for the life of them cannot perform, a result of the emotional state blocking any cognitive efforts or rational thought.

5.

Being hijacked will happen. When people hijack other peoples emotions they tend to go for the full monty, they want destruction and reaction. Your job and your team's (which you are teaching) is to strategize and stop your reaction and the reaction(s) of others-often anger, frustration, anxiety etc. Hijacking emotions happens when people trigger a soft spot, and they know it will 'move' you. Visualization often helps stop this if your thoughts stay focused and positive. Being aware and meta cognitive will help avoid outbursts.

You overall effort in learning EQ should be first on yourself then on others. Self-awareness is primary in the management of emotions. Study your trigger points, or buttons, that set off negative reactions and learn to control them. The more you know the more power you hold over yourself and leadership capabilities.

THE SEVEN

There seems to be a mystical association about this number, many things come in seven. The leadership pitfalls, called the seven, fall into seven categories. Robert Greene's book, mastery, mentions 7 deadly realities, there are 7 deadly sins-you get the picture.

Most people have these traits within themselves in one degree or another. Your job as a leader, is to focus on weeding these out of your life-some will take more time than others. You must end your tendencies to be envious, passive aggressive, wrathful, lazy, rigid ,self absorbed, conformist. Your path to minimizing these qualities will be hard work and it will take a lot of patience and trust in yourself to end these, if you are to truly lead.

Study and hard work are the sole solutions to these leadership career stallers. Any one of the seven listed can hurt your followers and your career as we will look into further.

Wrath/Anger (1/7)

This is a uncontrollable emotion that is irrational and is based on self interest and self indulgence. An easy example would be the display of anger that can be seen in children. They often burst out into anger over the simplest items and personal frustrations. Researchers define this as the warrior gene, where aggression and violence were the recipe for many problems that we faced as a species many years ago. Unfortunately in many cultural areas of the world we still see as the aggressor as a leader who can fix our problems via angry outbursts, an irrational behaviour.

Angry people separate themselves from reality. Behaviourists asses that the cognition of the self and the world stems from being based on interpretation and environmental interference. This means that outside factors will determine your reaction to what is happening and if you are able to handle it mentally. On the other end -will you, like a child lash out, because you do not understand your emotions and the situation, or stay composed and collected, mentally resolving the issue at hand.

> "Speak when you are angry and you will make the best speech you will ever regret."—Ambrose Bierce

Many people use anger to get results. There are managers who burst out of frustration but not only that use anger to get their point across, in order to make people understand their point or how serious the situation is. There are other ways of doing this and realizing your goals and desires.

But what is anger?

A broad range of writers and scientists agree that anger is a result of frustration. They do not stop there, they identify that anger is multidimensional with a clear affective and behavioural, as well as cognitive elements that contribute to the expression and experience of this emotion. You recall events that you were angry about very clearly, maybe not in whole detail but you remember them. The intensity of this emotion fuses to your memory and you can recall situation(s). That is why we get angry about things we got angry about before-taxes, global warming, child abuse, war etc. It is even more influential if as a result of our anger we got the results we wanted, amplifying our desire to use it.

In order to save yourself from this frustration you need to understand what sets you off. If your personal values and goals are dear to you and you have invested much effort and time in them, the inability to complete these goals will surely make you angry. Your understanding that things might not always go the way you planned is a strategy that will save you much tribulation. Or that there are people who will try to get in your way of your goals will inevitably save you time and frustration.

Not only are your goals important, values that you hold dear such as considering a insult, disrespect, threats to autonomy, your reputation can, all trigger a angry reaction. Your appraisal of situations will ultimately determine if you will become angry. No one can teach you these things, they are a part of you and you need to know how to identify and control your urge to react. The notion that something is violating your rules and norms is a precursor to the reaction of anger. When feeling that something is about to get 'touchy' in your world, is a good sign that you are about to get angry afterwards.

The group you are in or the cultural organization that defines what is right and wrong, both in behaviour and business determines your rules and values and how you will react. Citing Stanley Coren's book the intelligence of dogs on the subject of how groups influence the rules of behaviour:

(Explore)The difference between the hang-dog expression of the family dog when he does not get to go in the car and his angry growl when someone reaches for a bone in his mouth. The former reflects a disappointment -like state fuelled by a loss of his goal, while the latter reflects violation of its natural state and the universal rule where anything in the dogs mouth is its property, regardless of all other rules.

Your embodiment that others have acted wrongly against you or your values and goals elicits anger in some way. This is part of being human. However, your goals is not to eliminate anger but to channel it into civilized thought and reaction. This powerful emotion is present in all humans, it is a species flaw to the point it clouds judgment and reduces us to the animal state. The positive part of anger is that we can channel it to utilize it, instead of violence or troubling behaviour that is irrational, we can use it to fuel ambition and passion.

Coping in this state is a trained skill, a skill that is developed   by exposing yourself to failure. Many master's give their apprentices difficult tasks to fail in, in order to learn limitations and improve on skills. Failing is the fertilizer to success. Frustrations of failure lead to anger, know the reason behind this and you will avoid moronic blunders at work, school and life. Understanding how to lose is a important life skill.

"The best fighter is never angry."—Lao Tzu

Your mental muscle on yourself and your rules needs to be controlled. Say to yourself, that a reaction of rage and frustration will ultimately do you no good. However you look at it reacting in anger is so limited that it is reserved for children. To reach the heights of leadership your first step is to conquer anger. Marcus Aurelius wrote, "how much more grievous are the consequences of anger than the causes of it." Take the advice from the Roman emperor, and control your impulses.

Laziness (2/7)

If you wondered why many people are so poor in America, or Canada whilst the abundance of actual jobs you have answered your own question. Imagine the Sloth, an animal that is quite interestingly repulsive. By its own name we term a synonym for laziness. Moving slowly not a care in the world, not having much, not wanting much, it is the description of what poor performing is all about.

If you find this type of lifestyle fitting you should reconsider leadership. Leading requires work.

We now live in a society, where we idolize this type of behaviour. Why work hard and wait when we can use our credit cards to get what we want now. Why bother, we are all going to die anyways. Who wants to be exposed to more toil, ill stay in my couch thanks...

"Progress is made by lazy men looking for easier ways to do things."— Robert A. Heinlein

The future is trending towards producing more of this behaviour, your job is not going to be easy as the leader because of being lazy. Most of our problems that we encounter, relationship problems, financial, career etc are rooted in a form of laziness and procrastination. We lack energy and desire and passion. Most of all we lack motivation. We lack motivation in our work, in school and the results speak for themselves.

Motivation is as much understanding it as it is using it. I remember my high school teachers telling me "just try harder", "apply your self more". These words are meaningless as they do not explain why I need to try harder, those comments just piss people off and disengage them more. If you yourself do not know why you are doing something, the bother is too much to engage yourself.

An experiment was done on 7 girls and 13 boys to test the comments made by teachers to see if they could be swayed through motivation. The age ranged from 7 year olds to 10 year olds. No children that participated were diagnosed with a learning disability. The parents education levels ranged from half just finishing high school and the others completing higher qualifications. The results were surprising to say the least.

It was concluded that the 20 children who were interviewed and looked at, all of them had improper motivation. It was not the children's inability to learn or their disinterest in the subjects they were learning and it even wasn't the teachers that kept telling them the same old stories, it was the parents. The leaders of the family that unintentionally unmotivated the children when they failed at something. They built up a databank of failures to keep them from trying. Bad feedback or no feedback made the kids quit, and stop from trying at all.

You must know that your motivations might have this same databank. Erase it from your memory and start over, in your mind if you have to and you do in order to continue leading. Your motivation is the fuel that will power your leadership. Your followers cannot follow you if they themselves are lazy and unmotivated. Know that your expectations (and rewards) should be met with explanation and coaching. If someone screws up then show them the right way.

Never leave a conversation without positivity in the end. Leadership is not about driving people into the ground like nails, its about the nail wanting to drive itself out of its fee will- in. Laziness sort of makes the leader want to push people harder, sometimes that's ok, however, doing this too often will lead into negatively with your followers.

Ok, so now we know that part of being lazy is motivation but what else is involved? This is a subjective term and involves a lot of personal traits of individuals, motivation is not the only piece of laziness. While motivation plays its part, we live in a generation where everything is at our finger tips, and we know it!

The lack of interest in our lives is something previous generations would never have taken for granted. If we look only 100 years ago, we had to ride horses to get around. It took 3 weeks to cross the ocean, maybe longer. Who cares? You should, your mind is becoming soft with complacency each passing day. You think you have control but you don't, you get lured into other peoples plans, yours are too hard and you'll get around to it, is what you tell yourself. Your complacency and uninterested attitude will cost you years of catching up.

To change this behaviour you are imminently responsive to the present moment, planning and thinking of the future and past experiences do not do you any favours and promote procrastination. The immediate stimulation that you get from watching television or listening to music distracts you from thinking ahead thus weakening discipline. This fight, your fight to control the outside forces that want you to turn off your brain is constantly being fought. To not think and not plan. Nowadays as a society we want to be rewarded right away, even if it is satisfying our needs immediately instead of sitting down and studying for the exam weeks away. Immediate pleasure is a curse and you need to avoid it to stay sharp. Your followers are followers for a reason, they cannot control their impulses, they need someone to show them how to. That's you, its called self control, use it often.

Fight laziness the following ways:

1. Check yourself: Keep tabs on your plans and goals.

2. Commit to others: Its called integrity and your reputation is associated directly to it. Other peoples accountability makes you work.

3. Challenge yourself: Remember the kids experiment, give yourself the motivation if nobody else will. Your mostly on your own with the leadership development anyways.

4. Don't go too big: Start small and then go from there. Is it just 15min that needs to be done. You might even like what you start. Build discipline slowly.

5. Remember it's a process: Reward yourself for completing things, your laziness will disappear and motivation will no longer be a problem.

Lazy hands make for poverty, but diligent hands bring wealth.

Proverbs 10:4

Envy (3/7)

We are surrounded by individuals who display extraordinary skill and talent. We often find ourselves questioning the abilities we have with what they have. Comparisons, benchmarking whatever term you use the simple definition is envy.

Russell Bertrand mentioned that one of the biggest reasons people are unhappy is because of envy. Not only are you unhappy because you are envious of others but you are unhappy and wish misfortune on them as well.

Animals also display envy in the form of materialistic things, food. Monkeys who see other monkeys with their desired food will be envious of those monkeys and conspire to steal it. Charles Darwin in his theory of evolution (1859) rather natural selection, humans will behave in a way that amplifies their survival and the reproduction of their genes. This social behaviour envelops envy as the socio-cultural survival factor that motivates individuals to connive and ensure their survival.

The Red Slide

There are massive political systems that tried to eliminate envy and failed. The creation of communism tried to make everyone equal. The German born philosopher Karl Marx published The Communist Manifesto and Das Kapital in a effort to explain why there exists the haves and have nots. The class struggle as Marx concluded was a too wide a gap that existed. Capitalism produced an amplified effect on peoples struggles to be better than one another, he was hinting at eliminating envy of each other. There were times when both worked for short periods of time.

While the growth of communism rose after Marx, the ideals were flawed. Millions of people suffered under those regimes due to the exact principles they tried to eliminate. Envy still existed, on the government and government officials that ran the place(s). You cannot hold people to their devices and add rules to oppress them, they see the reality or the reality they want to see. On many levels of communist society envy existed.

"Resentment is like drinking poison and waiting for the other person to die."—Carrie Fisher

This oppression of the envious is present today. Leadership is a delicate flower that is in a war zone. A wrong move and you get blown away. Your ability to sense-make of what is going on will give you insight into seeing insecure individuals who are envious of you. Envy rises from the belief that we are not good enough. Society has blinded us with the onslaught of

84

media, we only see the end result, the gold medal. We do not see the toil and sweat and turmoil that came to that gold medal. Imagine you leadership as part of the Olympic training regiment, you must find and identify people who show an overly friendly attitude towards you, they are looking to dig information out of you, your first test is to know who you are dealing with.

Envious people are great chameleons and disguise themselves very well. Do not confuse envy with jealously. They are similar yet different. Jealousy involves the fear one has of losing someone or something that a person is attached to. Envy is the resentment that is caused because someone has something that we do not. Many chameleons do not know themselves if they are envious or jealous.

I mentioned it earlier that envy is a tricky behaviour. We see the end result. Your success that made you a leader (or to be leader) involves the hidden. People do not know what it took to get to where you are now. The sooner you realize this the better you will inevitably see people who are envious of you, by their petty complaints/irritations about you. The problems that arise from the fact that people see you as a aspiring leader where many follow. The envious place themselves in a mental cage that they cannot escape unless they undermine you and try to make you look bad, stupid, silly etc. They watch your every move looking for the chink in your armour and when they find it they will be merciless towards you. Envy will poison reason and rationality.

So how do you manage a screwed up perception of happiness and the envious? How do you convince someone that their way of assessing people and their own work is wrong?

Aristotle explained envy as "the pain caused by the good fortune of others". Organizations call this 'social comparison', it might be happening in your company and your team the pain in other words is envy. What this means is, if worker A is compensated via a bonus they might feel: relief, joy or anger. They will feel relief because they now fit in with the organizational group, joy when they know what they can buy with this bonus, and anger when they find out that others at the same level got paid more.

It is not uncommon to uncover that our peers are covertly conspiring against us, meddling with the boss in order to sway their decision about our image. When they compare us with themselves in the workplace, feelings of envy may arise.

You might of heard this chatter at the office cooler "why not me?" This is the social comparison that the perceiver elicits to themselves as being of the same level of competence and the injustice that occurred to them. This misery is in themselves to solve, your job is to get them away from you as their infectious nature will affect everyone around them.

Envy has been around for quite some time and much has been written about it. Religions around the world preach against it. The book of Genesis shows us two brothers that offered a sacrifice to God, God favoured Able's sacrifice over Cain's. Cain ended up killing Able because of it. The fact that this is one of the first things that the Bible teaches Christians puts significant importance on Envy as being a sinful and foolish. It is hard however, not to compare ourselves with others, comparing does not turn into envy if its not malicious.

There is a positive side to envy. It can be used as a positive motivational force. This benign form of envy should be used as assessment, and shouldn't be called envy (we mentioned envy as being resentful and intending to hurt). You should call this measurement. If someone who is similar to us in physical and mental means as well as financial is having more success, then it is not them but us that need to change. Leaderships many definitions involve the adaptations of the leader and that is what a successful leader should be doing. To become successful adapt to your superior that is more successful than you. Read the chapter on Humility for more.

The antidote to envy, if we are experiencing it is joy for the good fortune of others. No matter how unfair life is to us. Nicomachean ethics teaches us that to be part of the supreme good which is part of the rational soul, we need to behave in a right manner both in extreme times of deficiency and in excess. This behaviour in the end gets rewarded via, promotions, raises, bonuses etc.

"Envy consists in seeing things never in themselves, but only in their relations. If you desire glory, you may envy Napoleon, but Napoleon envied Caesar, Caesar envied Alexander, and Alexander, I daresay, envied Hercules, who never existed."Bertrand Russell

Rigidity (4/7)

"Notice that the stiffest tree is most easily cracked, while the bamboo or willow survives by bending with the wind."

Bruce Lee

We are the products of our own demise. With the business environment going global and increasing complexity of all processes, everything is trying to grab a hold of us, we must hold onto what we know. We stick with old ideas and methods of work. We hang out with like minded people. We fear change, it involves too much work to change again. We are rigid.

Try to introduce a new procedure to your team and you'll see what happens. They will not advertise this rigidity. I have had many examples of introducing myself to a new group of associates with, "here is how we are going to do things going forward", didn't work out so well. The change effort involved is too much for people to handle. Some quit, others rebel. being flexible to them means expending more energy due to the personal commitment to the change.

You goal is to let go of old ideas and embrace the new ones. You cannot change the rigidity in others lest they change themselves. If you hold veto power you can only explain why you are doing something, maybe its for more money in their pockets. This will quell their rebellious nature for a while. Mental limitations due to inexperience enforce rigidity.

The Nemean lion from Greek mythology shows a beast that is unstoppable, the fur impenetrable from any mortal weapons. Heracles the hero who eventually slays the lion, tries to skin the fur using his sword, and other sharp objects to no avail. Most would leave and give up, but he kept trying new things, but still he had no luck in breaking the skin. The goddess Athena finally told him to use the own lion's claw to skin it and it worked. Fluidity and flexibility have their rewards.

> "There is no such thing as bad weather, only inappropriate clothing."— German Proverb

You ability to stay motivated and flexible to different options is much like Heracles trying his ways of skinning the beast. The tools and skills you have might not be the ones that you are supposed to be using to solve your problems. You should be looking around you, what you have at your disposal, your team, your environment, your experience to push through the challenge. Much like the claw there are always hidden solutions in a opportunity if you look hard enough. But to do that you cannot be concrete, you must be sand-easily adaptable.

The Red Slide

In more than a decade of fighting and unsuccessful battles, Rome needed a new leader to control the advancing tribes. Gaius Marius was that necessary leader. Marius the roman general was the last hope for Rome against the barbarian tribes that decimated Rome.

Rigidity has many forms, in our observation of the Roman empire they were accustomed to being the ones who were attacking and having their enemies fleeing. They were not known to being on the defensive, the solutions they had were placing 'political' leaders to deal with the barbarians, but these leaders did not have the intuition and flexibility that the fight required. The barbarians did not follow any conventional styles of fighting they just fought. The Romans finally selected Gaius to clear them out, as being a leader in the field he knew that he could not fight the enemy on any conventional tried and tested ways; he needed to think outside the box and adapt to the enemy. We often in our lives do as the Romans did, use old ways to try to make new things.

Passive aggression (5/7)

In psychology, passive aggression is a disorder. Experts describe it as a pattern formed from habits that resist expectations. We are passive aggressive because we do not want to do the work, we oppose our leaders, we are stubborn and we are negative. All of this for the expectation of normal requirements yet you as the leader will be asked for extraordinary requirements.

This attitude or behaviour is a result of amplified media presence and socio-cultural misguidance in our society today. The amount of 'get rich quick schemes' we get exposed to either in our internet lives or on tv-through reality television is a direct result of our delusional selves thinking we can do the same. We play the passive aggressive game in order to exert as little effort as possible while trying to get the maximum results.

Millenials are notorious for passive aggressiveness, their education and upbringing was a result of unrealistic and cloudy media teaching. Even in cartoons and children's shows we teach our children that they can have anything they want. The children will one day be adults, and their hard to kick habits will result in your extra work in leading them.

There was a study of two types of fish in a single aquarium, one was prey and one was the predator. The only thing that separated them was a piece of glass in the middle, they could still see each other through the glass. The predator fish constantly kept banging on the glass trying to eat the prey fish, which were swimming on the farthest side of the aquarium trying to get away. After some time, the predator fish figured out that it could not get the prey, and they prey figured out that the predator could not get them either. This is not the interesting part. After seeing this behaviour the scientists took the glass away from the middle of the tank, leaving it fair game. What happened, was what we call learned apathy. The predator did not venture over to the prey's side and vice versa. They gave up! Both of them, they figured that it couldn't be done so why bother.

Learned apathy is part of passive aggressiveness, why try when we "know" we are going to fail and we know others will too. Its too much work to get started, ill wait for someone else to go and then ill join we tell ourselves. Society makes it so that we must be passive aggressive, and indirectly place invisible glass in front of us to teach us learned apathy. After all leadership is not for everyone. Apathy multiplies passive aggression by indulging in ignorance, which is brought onto us from others.

The passive aggressive conflict cycle

Written by Whitson, the PACC is an interesting way of looking at passive aggression. The five steps that are involved explain why sometime rational adults lose control of themselves and cause a unprofessional atmosphere. Here are the parts that make it up:

Part 1: Self beliefs and personal image- The person from a variety of life experiences has learned to hide their anger through clever remarks and manipulative behaviour. They get a high on thinking themselves more intellectually powerful than others as they masquerade their true feelings. We see this form in people in power.

Part 2: Stress-When a passive aggressive person is asked to do something their mental model tells them the following. "I have to do everything here", "They are always using me for this stuff", "Ill get them back and they will not see it coming". Pushing their anger below the skin as not to induce detection believing showing anger is unacceptable. This can be in a person that has been disciplined or is on performance issues.

Part 3: Feelings-Passive aggressive people through their life experiences have learned to hide negative feeling from society and project them in a different form. They are passive aggressive because they do not know how to express them otherwise, leaving a trail of carnage behind them without them caring or noticing.

Part 4: Behaviour- This behaviour is intentional and serves a purpose to the aggressor. The purpose is expression of ones feelings by throwing others off their game. Getting back through passive aggression to them is fair game.

> "Anger is an acid that can do more harm to the vessel in which it is stored than to anything on which it is poured."—Mark Twain

Part 5: Reactions from others- The main reaction is anger from others that come in contact with passive aggression. Typically people who often are cheery and calm get side swiped by an aggressor and their 'comments'.

Your role as a leader of the group is two things. First, do not be passive aggressive yourself, you need to express your feelings to someone you trust and have courage to discuss difficult situations. Second, identify passive aggressors and confront their behaviours before they un ravel the whole team. Seek professional help if this is your boss.

In the Bill Clinton era, there was a time that we could say he was displaying a passive aggressive behaviour with the scandal of womanizing and on top of it lying about it on national television. Even the highest status leaders are not immune to the term. The mental model of Clinton at the time was that he was untouchable and could get away with it, passive aggressive individuals want it all without the consequences and its always someone else's fault. It is often when the facts are thrown at PA they admit to their actions.

Conformism (6/7)

Leadership and conformism are not supposed to be in the same sentence. It does happen in leadership, more often than we think. The leader is beat down by the every day drudgery that happens and loses motivation to make a difference. The result is that they give up and start to desire a norm of behaviours that will not rock the boat so much. Peer pressure and the agitation that is received by implementing something the leader gets exhausted and eventually makes himself exposed and a victim of conformism and complacency.

We learn to conform in our early childhoods. Children often want to fit in and play with others so they follow the lead of the group. To be different means social punishment and embarrassment. This feeling eventually sticks with us into our teens as the pressure to follow trends gets even greater. To be part of the 'cool' kids we again play the game of fitting in. By this time we have been conformists for the most of our lives and its becoming natural to camouflage ourselves to society and its demands. As adults we keep conforming to our boss, our company and our society.

"To be yourself in a world that is constantly trying to make you something else is the greatest accomplishment."
—Ralph Waldo Emerson

Besides courage, to break away from conformism we must acknowledge that we are weak and scared of what might happen. We are afraid of the unknown, and will do anything to stay in our safe zone. Publicly agreeing to a group when you know something is not right is conformism with a touch of tainted integrity. As professionals we need to know that our opinions matter to the group. Maybe you found something that others have overlooked, and by keeping quiet you actually hurt the group, not help 'collaboration'.

Speaking your mind is important in the context of what is going on. If you are talking about forecasting next year's budgets then don't talk about the game, talk about budgets, conforming just to make the other person comfortable when the time is not right is a waste of time. This group phenomenon, factors in the group size (the bigger the group the more you will conform), status, prior commitments and public opinions. These factors add to the conformist attitude you want to avoid.

Yet we see this form of rational acquiescence from all members of society. The notion of rebellion and the harm it could inflict on society, the economy and us personally makes us consent to the rules of our times. We believe in justice, and that any wrongs that happen, the law will take care of them. We believe that conforming in the eyes of society will help us not hurt us. Yet, we still see successful people who step outside the box (not breaking any rules) and we admire them. These people can only be conformists if in the legal sense. They are rebellious in their mind and will not be pinned down to rules of organizational conformity and status quo.

What I want you to understand is that it is your duty as a socially responsible citizen to follow all the rules of society. If you are feeling like you are conforming your self-reflection should provide some answers. Do not comply on the notion that you did everything you could. I can hear my mother repeating my words while I was in high school looking at my terrible report card "but you tried you best?!". The best is not good enough, you are taught to keep your thoughts and ideas to yourself. Break the habit of thinking that it is out of your power and realize that you will be the maker of your own path.

Think of conformism as theft of the mind. If someone was to steal your wallet how would you react when you found them. Probably call the police or beat them to a pulp. What if then, society is stealing your mind and you are allowing them to? What if you are a great leader but you just don't realize it? You need to get

96

back at society and show people that you are the leader you know you are.

Self absorption (7/7)

The only thing standing in front of the Roman way of life and the invasion of Italy was the volunteer militia called the Roman army. Priding itself in the organization, training and discipline it saw itself as superior to anything that existed at the time. The officials in the Roman senate were the ones who made the decisions, and first priority was national security. Much of the decision making was about politics, legislation and reforms that needed to be done in order to keep the empire growing and sustain it. However, with the expansion and growth come many hidden characteristics of a crumbling system. Corruption alongside with wealth started to take away from the political process of Roman democracy and the need for reforms.

The leadership that was in that day displayed was through war and warfare. Any decisions that happened had one form of battle in it. The display of manliness so to speak was to go and fight. Self absorption causes many of us to think that we are unbeatable and indestructible much like the Romans thought. The truth is very different.

The Red Slide

Beyond the roman territories lay a formidable adversary to the empire of Ancient Rome. They called them barbarians and they were nothing like the warriors of before. To the Romans the barbarians were crude and foreign, an unorganized group of fighters that threatened the peace in the empire, they were as dangerous as they were resilient.

They viewed the barbarians as much less civilized and much less intellectually equal than themselves. Anyone that did not speak in the custom way of Roman society, either Latin or Greek they were viewed as different, awkward and uncivilized. This meant that you either followed Roman law and tradition or risk being ostracized, sometimes for good.

Thinking ourselves untouchable creates many enemies that otherwise we could have done without.The Cimbri barbarians that were betrayed in a peace negotiation by the roman general and counsel Carbo, swore that they would never leave until the fall of Rome happened. The amateur hour for a new general and his leadership often results in disaster like Carbo, we think too highly of ourselves and we cannot see the snakes hiding in the grass. The Roman generals facing the Cimbri were in this pot of self-absorption.

We have an example of a Roman exception, the Roman general Marius who was the polar opposite of Carbo. Humble, battle tested, eating and digging the ditches with his soldiers and some say was in better shape than his men, and they were the most physically fit soldiers in the world. Marius fought on what is now present day

The Red Slide

Algeria, then called Numidia. Winning that long campaign was among his many successes as a Roman as his success over the Numidian King Jugurtha made him a valid candidate to take on the Barbarians in the north. To read more on Marius look at rigidity (flexibility) as a leader.

The next several centuries for the roman empire being in a state of self-absorption as a society would wreak havoc for the empire eventually falling and crumbling from within. The lesson for you and your leadership is that you are never too smart, too strong, too rich or too important. The pride comes before the fall, it was true for the Roman empire and so it is with you.

Your followers want to see what you stand for, and if they are caught in self absorbed behaviours then it is up to you to put them in check. Your success depends on your identification of how to take control of flimsy delusions of grandeur. In the end, Carbo disgraced by his performance as a leader commits suicide for dishonouring himself, his family and the empire. While Marius get voted to counsel a record 7 times.

We often find out until its too late, that we are our own worst enemies and its in self absorption that this happens. Our past success makes us blind to the fact that they are just that, the past. We get a notion of being unstoppable, much like the roman's in their arrogance against the barbarians. We might think we are dealing with barbarians ourselves in our lives and this will undo any hard work that you have done until now, as it takes a few moments of arrogance and ignorance to spell your failure.

LEADERSHIP CLARITY THROUGH HUMILITY

"True humility is not thinking less of yourself; it is thinking of yourself less." C.S. Lewis

Most employees in organizations want to feel safe that their leader is in control, displays power and charisma. These common traits are seen in executives often. humility is hard to quantify as it is hard to measure leaders who prefer not to talk about themselves, whereas their loud, charismatic and highly visible counter parts are easily figured out.

Jedidiah was the son of David in the old testament, more famously known as King Solomon. During his 40 year reign of the Israelite monarchy, the Hebrew kingdom experienced its greatest wealth. He was a builder, politician, sage, and the leader of the Hebrews in a time of uncertainty and tribulation. Some claim that King Solomon was the richest person who ever lived. So how is it that a person such as Solomon took the time to write a 'how to guide' to living. This guide is today followed by more than 3 world leading religions. Although his riches and wealth were evident, the action to transfer his knowledge to others is what people remember him by.

Leaders such as Solomon are aware of what they accomplished and can accomplish. It is however a different story of what they will do with their accomplishments. Will you share what you have learned from your mentors and teachers and bestow this knowledge to your apprentice and managers? Humbleness is not just looking in the mirror, the importance of our thoughts is second to the thoughts of what needs to be solved.

We do not look in the mirror but look outside the window, to the toils of our colleagues who helped us achieve these results. Humbleness can be seen in other people who always put their neighbours, wives, husbands, kids and supervisors ahead of themselves.

Many view humility as a weakness, it is often the opposite. History has proven to us that the humble general who does not flaunt his strength and is pulled back emotionally, often has the upper hand. Other call this retreat, it is however a very useful leadership and management strategy. The leader who humbles himself in front of a situation that is escalating and avoids conflict is actually trading something. They trade the situation they are in for the time they need to figure out a better strategy.

> "A true genius admits he/she knows nothing." — Albert Einstein

Strategic humility can be seen in Taoism. Taoism was built on the philosophy of wei wu (action through inaction). The three treasures of wei wu-are compassion, moderation and humility. The only way a leader can clearly see the obstacles ahead of him and the dangers they possess is by stepping back and taking a look from the top of the roof. Do not act on the first sign of danger. Not acting when everyone else is, gives you perspective on how things are going. Not reacting when everyone is screaming, focuses you on the problems of the conflict.

Humility requires you to respond to situations not react. Reactions are emotionally attached and often ridiculous. Response takes time. Wei Wu your way to a proper decision. Do not be a mechanical entity that computes decisions. We do this because we are influenced by the copious amounts of television and reality shows that we watch, and romanticize the same reactive behaviours we see on television. The initial emotional reactions that we give out are primal in nature, humility requires patience which is not a primal characteristic but a evolutionary one.

Two countries in World War I were at war in East Africa. On the English side was Lt. General Jan Smuts, a man used to winning most of his life and one who does not back down from a fight. On the German side was Colonel Paul von Lettow-Vorbeck, a very clever and dedicated German national. Lettow-Vorbeck was determined to keep as many British troops away from the western front by tying them down any way he knew how. Smuts was calculating a fast win over the smaller German force, but von Lettow-Vorbeck avoided any confrontation and retreated south. Smuts kept pursuing wanting to engage in combat, however, the German colonel kept retreating until the supply lines for the British were thinned out and their morale destroyed. This cat and mouse game lasted for four years, the British learned their lesson, and were eventually beaten through exhaustion.

Your ability to pull back and let nature take its course when met with aggression is a learned trait. Anger is instinctual and most people do not know this until it is too late. Anger clouds judgment and reason. Humility heightens judgment and gives us time to think of solutions. Coupled with other negative emotions, such as envy, anger will make the leader give out poor decisions and hasty ones that cannot be over turned. The results taint and isolate the leader.

In the whirlwind of daily life and work-you must fight to separate yourself from your initial infecting emotional influences. Humbleness helps you do this. Remind yourself that you need time, and you are not in a hurry. Mentally slap yourself when you feel the need to boast or place your name on the title page. The initial gratification that you get, even if you did do most of the work will cause a mountain of resentment from your peers.

"True humility does not know that it is humble. If it did, it would be proud from the contemplation of so fine a virtue."— Martin Luther

There are other qualities that humbleness gives. We often overlook the trap that zealous action does to us. We live in a 'now' society, and we want everything now. Results now, money now, promotion now , victory now etc. Your goal is to balance yourself and separate the whirlwind from you.

Only the best leaders have the ability to be humble and effective. They do not try to boast or fill the room with their presence, it is felt regardless with a calm demeanour and discipline. Young leaders need to practice patience and being humble even if it is for exercises sake, just to see if they can do it. If you cannot act being a humble leader for a month then it is evident you don't have the maturity to hold your emotions in check. Even acting humble enables better results than a pompous posturing leader.

To practice humility in our everyday lives we need to shut off the tv and distractions. The images and songs that we hear infect our reason, in that belligerent and obnoxious behaviour will trump all others.

Clarify what it is you need to do and learn as a emerging leader and mentor. Clarify what you are, what your goals are, and what you stand for. In Catholicism, the greatest example of humility is in the form of a baby being born in a manger, with Jesus Christ being the son of God you would think a 5 star hotel would do no less. The virtue of humility is not by chance in the Bilble and other religions. It is the quality to which all others should follow, humility enables many followers of Catholicism, Islam, Taoism, Buddism and others to reach a state of higher cognition in order to communicate with their subconscious and seek guidance. With this internal talk we can plan, strategize and execute seemingly difficult problems through our creativeness. It is easier to be creative when you are free of distractions, being humble gives you more peace to think.

We romanticize and admire humility in others, however, we do not practice it ourselves. How much more followers we would have if we followed humbleness. Who does not like someone who helps us and does not request anything in return. Leaders who exemplify these qualities have much more respect and buy in from their followers because they do what it takes to win over their followers and not neglect them.

There is another term for humility in leadership, it is called servanthood. Starting in Arkansas , USA and still going now, the worlds largest retailer and the legacy of Sam Walton still lives on, as a servant to the community and his employees. Sam Walton knew that he needed the people in his company to make it successful and this mentality ensured that he didn't take them for granted. If you want to know how to influence people, learn from Sam. Be there for your people, listen to them, care about what they have to say and then take the time to do something about it.

Humbleness is inspirational to your followers. So don't beat the same drum everyday and avoid micromanagement, you are not the smartest person in the room (even if you are, avoid showing it). They know and see your responsibilities and what you must do day in and day out. Why do you think you need to remind them everyday? You don't, micromanagement is not inspirational. They know. Get over yourself. The inspiration comes from moving on and making them successful, investing time and patience in working on their faults without acknowledging their faults. Andrea Bocelli became fully blind at age 12, his optimism and humble spirit enables him to keep creating and singing musical masterpieces that millions envy and aspire to become. What would you do if you became blind now? How will you act and behave? Would you inspire or conspire because of your circumstances?

Religion played a role in the making of many humble leaders. Many of them unaware of the impact they would have for mankind with their refusal to acknowledge themselves as leaders, even though they were. Pietro di Bernardone's son Francis was born in 1186 at a time when the skepticism of the Catholic church was at a all time high. Francis made it clear that to live a godly life, one must serve and ignore the hierarchical orders that society brings on people. Francis of Assisi (as we know him today) made it a priority to putting the poor and sick on his main obligations. This moral leadership is becoming rare today. This leadership that Francis made, gave him the tools to be successful in that time, more than any bishop or general that lived.

"Humility means accepting reality with no attempt to outsmart it." —David Richo

The fight against yourself and your selfish desires is next to sainthood in many aspects of theological philosophy. There is something that we fantasize about people who give up everything to serve the poor, we say to ourselves, "I can appreciate that." , but we would never do it! Why is that? The sacrifice and the venturing into the unknown is what scares us into complacency and stagnation. Francis's friends would joke at him and ask "when will you marry?", his answer was "my only bride from now on will be lady poverty.". Francis would continue to serve in poverty until the end of his days. In leadership we sometimes need to live in poverty (figuratively) to eventually get the glory.

The problem with humility is that it is difficult to replicate and transfer to your followers. Proving that giving gets more than taking is hard for people to see. Francis had a similar problem, how was he going to convince his followers to go on the same path as him (relinquish all worldly possessions) at the same time convince the Pope that he was not making a cult. At a time when corruption was eminent in the Catholic Church the pope needed leaders such as Francis who embodied the life of Jesus, his actions were approved. Qualities such as humility are not desirable in a world where we live on material restrictions, bills, new trends etc. All things to keep up with the 'Joneses' restrict a humble attitude.

Humility also does something that many people do not notice, humble people are often very intelligent and make very intelligence choices. The ability to calm your mental thoughts while in crisis gives you're a clear picture of the battlefield. Deceptions of grandeur cloud judgment and give you a false sense of strength. How many times did we underestimate that jar of pickles, thinking it would open with a simple twist, in

---

the end giving 'er all we got to open the jar. The truth is that many of us do not practice humility and this is a result of the environment we live in.

Our goal is not to reach sainthood (unless you really want to), your goal is to lower yourself to realism. At anytime in your life, and probably more than once, you can lose it all. Things go wrong, you are flying high one minute the next you are in the ditch. Learn to be humble and the environment (call it the universe/spirit/god whatever) will accept your gratitude and leave you be.

Cut throats at work, banks playing with our money, global economy in shambles, politicians promising everything but the promise, world war on the horizon. Why should we practice humility? We need to get ours? This is the reason why many cannot be leaders and why many are found to be poor leaders, is because the realization of a short life that will be unfulfilled scares us. In leadership the fulfillment lies in how many people we can help and the journey we are on, not the size of the paycheque at the end of the day.

Leadership effectiveness does not come from what you take but from what you give.

Saint Francis of Assisi was at 5000 followers, two years after starting his movement. He stepped back and let others do the important HR and operations things, he kept to his word of living in poverty and serving. This historical example is what we should learn from, if we say we are going to do something we should do it, and if we need clarity of thought we need to practice humility.

"I went to the woods because I wished to live deliberately, to front only the essential facts of life, and see if I could not learn what it had to teach, and not, when I came to die, discover that I had not lived. I did not wish to live what was not life, living is so dear; nor did I wish to practice resignation, unless it was quite necessary. I wanted to live deep and suck out all the marrow of life...to drive life into a corner, and reduce it to its lowest terms.

-Henry David Thoreau-

HARDINESS AND STRESS CONTROL

Think back to when you were a kid, starting to go to school. Grade 1, your were met with many changes, homework, teachers holding you accountable, making new friends etc. Then you go used to it and everyone in that class. Then Grade 2, change again, harder homework, more of it. Then you got used to that. Then guess what, the cycle repeated itself until you finished high school. You are more used to change and you are more resilient than you think.

Hardiness or toughness is exercised stress. You get tougher by exercising your muscles, going to the gym, running every morning etc. You exercise your hardiness and mental toughness by exposing (intentionally or not) to life's exercises. More often than not you fail miserably the first time new (even the nth time) exercises come around. Most people give up after the first try. The change is too much, physically or mentally and they stop. Your dependence on your abilities makes you weak and stresses you out. You should rely on your mental matter rather than what your body tells you. Remember that you had to get

"We have not journeyed all this way because we are made of sugar candy."— Winston S. Churchill

through grade 1 or you would have been held back, you had no choice right? Well think of success the same way. You either go all in or flop.

Being good at leadership starts at a figurative grade 1, learning to read and learn leadership all the way to grade 12, what Jim Collins calls level 5 leadership. If to build hardiness we need to experience life and learn from it why don't we have more great leaders around us. There is no simple answer to this, but I will try: leadership isn't for everyone! Reading about leadership is easy, doing it is hard.

Contrary to what people want you to believe that stress is bad, its not. Its bad for the people who want it to be bad. Their mental maturity has not reached its focal point. You don't see too many CEO's committing suicide do you? They have the most stressful jobs on the planet, their decisions dictate economies. So why do you stress out? You have money problems? Stop drinking and smoking, sell your car and buy a cheaper one until you can afford a new one etc. Popular culture entices us that we are stressed about this and that, we see it everywhere and this brings down our self esteem about ourselves and psyches us out into thinking that we really might be stressed. You are not, you're tougher than that.

Only a small portion of today's leaders turn disasters into growth opportunities, the ones that do are very successful. According to Maddi, who coined the term Hardiness, there are three C's to a hardy attitude:

1. The first C- Challenge. You see and accept that life by its nature is stressful, and from this stressful situations are opportunities for growth and you take this and turn them into advantages. Learning not ignoring. You learn from both sides of the coin, success or failure you learn on both fronts. You don't quit because quitting is beneath you.

2. The second C is Commitment. Your attitude towards life is that regardless of how terrible things are getting you stay involved in the situation, rather than cowering and detaching yourself from everything and everyone.

3. The third Control. You believe that even in hopeless situations you learn to believe in trying to get the disaster into a growth opportunity.

The opposite of hardiness and you will see this in many people around you is denial and avoidance. This behaviour is categorized by people who escape their stressful situations by substance abuse, addiction, gambling, overspending and other impulsive behaviours. Resilience is what you are after, not indulgence, leave that for your last years when your 100 to indulge. Life is too short for you to take slow, the opposite of hardy is simply said being a "couch potato".

Imagine a child who is learning to dress themselves. What would happen if the parent who is teaching the child kept saying, "you'll never learn, that's not how you do that!", and they said this every time the child made a mistake. Besides locking up the parent for being a jerk, this kills the self esteem of the child. Future events will be determined by simple things such as this. The talent that this child, now a teenager or adult will never ultimately use because of the fear of failure. After all our parents know best, but they don't. After all our friends know best, but they don't. Our politicians know best, definitely don't.

Hardiness is about you, can you take failure can you manage stress and the unforeseen. Can you erase you past misconceptions and start new. Its hard and many cannot, and don't try. They psyche themselves out of action before even taking a single step, they need to see someone else do it before they do.

NURTURE CREATIVITY

In the movie business the success of a movie depends on the uncertain plot or unexpected idea's that the writers and directors take a look at. The best movies are the ones that the audience has no idea what will happen. The management however, makes a reluctant agreement to some of these story lines as they are huge gambles if they are going to be a success.

The leaders job is to let go of what they want to see happen and empower and encourage their teams to get going with innovation. This is the tough part of leadership, how do you organize a group of people with their own ways of doing things and thinking and getting them to get along with one another. The trust and respect that is required among the teams is something that the managers or leaders cannot put a mandate on. The things that we can do is to create a surrounding that encourages trust, respect and gives everyone to voice their ideas. This way everyone has their chance to give their input on what should be done, fair play, if an idea goes through the members all had a chance to contribute their views and a vote got the best one out.

"Others have seen what is and asked why. I have seen what could be and asked why not." —Pablo Picasso

One of the hardest parts for a leader to do will be to hire people who are smarter than they are. You will face decisions on individuals who are much more talented and intellectually superior to yourself. If you are afraid of losing your job, don't. You will look like a Don King who has a nose for the best talent in the industry, something which leadership is struggling with today. Be known for hiring the best most talented and creative folks and your future will be written in stone.

To solve problems at the executive and middle management level, you need to think out side the box(s). The competition is aggressively moving against your best product and service and you have limited time to get a new version out. Innovation and creativity cannot be sullied by the suits in offices, who are taught to think about nothing but short term profiting and early retirement.

Imagine children, when they are young they find the craziest ideas work. They use food to paint, creatively creating their world as they see fit. It only get suppressed when they start to follow rules that are either, obsolete, old, naive etc. It is a blessing to hire people outside your industry, they might have enough skills in an area where they worked before and they bring this into your field, a hybrid creator who looks for flaws in process. More often than not they work out. Perspective is everything.

"You can never solve a problem on the level on which it was created."— Albert Einstein

116

You manage to organize a team that can get ideas going. Like we talked about organizing them will be a issue if leadership is not cognizant of the talent that it has. You agenda should be to stir things up, encourage failure even reward it, the same with success. You punish only those that are inactive and fall in a complacent groove of work-life. If you are trying to create a competitive product or service your agenda needs to be pumping out ideas and testing them. Look at Edison's quote, you chose to fail only if you want to.

Persistence overcomes resistance, this saying is true in innovation. One of the main challenges in economics and macroeconomic development in business is the differences in performance on a national, regional and cultural level. Compare China 30 years ago with the US- a vast difference in production, quality of life, education and the whole myriad of differences. Now China has surpassed the US in almost everything except for air pollution. When you have no choice and your back is against the wall (figuratively speaking) you must re-create and re invest and re invent the wheel. Countries that are suffering in a rut of economic inactivity are stricken by fear-from their politicians or people. The only saving grace to any of these countries is not their resources but their human capital and what to do with that capital.

Creativity and innovation does not stop in business and governments, look at sports. Any sport you pick will show examples of innovation. LeBron James, the most mentioned basketball player in the world must adjust his playing style every year in order to stay competitive. Whether it's a new way of making a jump shot or cutting in the lane to get his lay ups the approach is the same, test, review and repeat until its right.

Leadership is much the same at the personal level. Your outcome as a leader will depend on the ability to identify trends and adapt to them. The creative network that you mingle with, including your own cognition, will help you add skills that are needed in your changing industry. Properties that are required to stay competitive you will see ahead of time. You do this by keeping a open mind to foreign ideas, foreign cultures, strange conversation and constantly developing yourself.

The interaction between humans is unique in that we can mimic and adapt and adjust to our own vision. Having creativity is also seeing an idea and putting our own flare to it. Toilet paper is white, but you see companies selling purple, blue, pink for some reason. The idea is the same, but you can add your taste to a already great idea to make it successful.

Remember that fear will stop you if you are to become a expert in creativity. We talked about fear in previous chapters. Your style of leadership will need to embrace fear and uncertainty and truly believe it in your teams that they can bring in a new industry changing idea. The courage that you display needs to be genuine or else people will see through your muse.

Innovation is a process that develops, and developing includes failure. The trick is how much can you endure without giving in to hopelessness. Imagine saying that you are going to need to create a vacuum that can RPM at 1,000milles an hour. People would laugh at you! Nowadays, that vacuum company is produces the most famous vacuums on the planet, the Dyson. Amazing things can happen when the leader is involved and has faith in the team, who never gives up no matter what the obstacles are in front of him.

"Maybe its just in America, but it seems that if you're passionate about somethings, it freaks people out. You're considered bizarre or eccentric. To me, it just means you know who you are."—Tim Burton

TWO ENDS OF THE SAME GOAL: MEDIOCRITY AND EXCELLENCE

Be careful how you define excellence as you will travel in that direction. On one path you will travel a road of confusion where you think excellence means perfection, its not. The other road is more realistic and involves commitment instead of any management cliché saying for getting people to do their jobs better. Your goal is to move towards commitment and understanding of being excellent in whatever you do, it is a pipe dream to look for perfection. Your strategy in this approach needs to be right, if you get it wrong you will be chasing shiny rocks that waste your time.

In the end of the 5th century BC, Sparta and Athens ended a long war in which Athens lost. In this time existed great thinkers, the likes of Socrates and writer such as Xenophon. Xenophon was special in that he tried to write a biography of the king of the Persians Cyrus the Great. Cyrus was a special kind of ruler for that time and he made quite an impression on history which we still study today.

Cyrus had a interesting childhood, able to travel around the world and spend time in luxury and wealth. These things, according to Xenophon, did not interest Cyrus. He was more interested in ruling and what the 'law' really meant to the people he would rule. He also saw that excellence can only be grasped by pushing limits and that no man is limited to their family tree but to the limits they set themselves. Some pretty profound thought for those days. Cyruses methods are debatable in the sense that he was good to the ones who were obedient and punished the 'law breakers'.

In his pursuit to compile the ideal constitution, a governing body that would ensure all would have a chance to excel, he mentions:

We are different from slaves in that slaves serve their masters unwillingly, but for us, if indeed we think we are free, it is necessary to do everything willingly which we think is worthwhile to do.

Xenophon tried to shape the thoughts surrounding a torn continent at the time of conservatism and innovation. Being conservative by formalizing social norms and hierarchical structures and being innovative by giving the people the choice to choose the best man for the job. It is however, a misrepresented story from Xenophon that Cyrus was in fact a manipulator of his people by offering financial rewards.

"I i cannot do great things, I can do small things in a great way."—Martin Luther King Jr.

They story of Cyrus, although not explained thoroughly enough by me and by Xenophon shows how stopping the learning process will turn off excelling at something. Even if Cyrus had the best intentions in the beginning of his life, the outside influences that he let happen turned his reason into manipulation and fear. This misuse of power is what many new managers and leaders insusceptibly fall into.

Imagine the sea, it has so many forms, only which the most skillful sailors dare to test. Even when the sea is playful it becomes deadly. Testing any person who decides they are up for a challenge. Now imagine your leadership world as the sea, and you, the new leader the sailor. What skills do you have to survive in this perfidious environment.

In your quest to reach the ultimate leadership level, the ultimate sailor. You will be met with loneliness, isolation and maybe even despair. You should not be a fatalist, trying not to be a pessimist as well but to know that resilience is the key to your success. That the process of excellence is filled with failing.

How do you become better at what you need to become better at. Practice. After that you do some more practice then you study others and then you practice their techniques.

Boxing has a interesting approach to excellence (in the ring). Its called shadow boxing, the boxer practices in front of a mirror and 'boxes' with themselves to see their form. Each punch is seen and adjusted until it goes right. Then it is done again until it becomes second nature. Excellence comes with much practice and investigation on your part.

You want to be a better leader? Expose yourself to situations that will force you to make leadership choices. Announce a meeting that you will lead even though your public speaking skills suck. Develop the uncomfortable skills that you own and make them better.

It is a systematic delivery system that increases leadership capability through your self management. We talked about emotional intelligence and self awareness, you pursuit of excellence is personal and should involve you and your follies and faults. Emotional, physical, psychological and any other traits that hold you back need to be fixed and muscled up.

This area of leadership would explain why so many dabble in leadership and there are so many that are ineffective. The need for future leaders will increase with the changes that are happening globally. Will you be there to meet the challenges. The importance of leadership ability is to change yourself which is part of excelling at change. I remember when the time of e-commerce demanded immediate changes both in the operations piece of the business but also in the whole business, it was get on or get off (permanently).

Your excellence development starts with a comparison journey. If you kept a diary the last couple of years great. Refer to it to see how you have changed. The things that stayed the same would probably need change. You need to compare yourself to yourself, your unique position right now in history will not be repeated and needs to be compared by you only. Do lists, graphs, you tube videos, whatever you think will help you identify weakness.

Once the weakness is seen, you need to read and find out what is causing it. Feedback from peers and people you feel comfortable with will ensure that you get the right information.

Excellence and the Pareto Principle

Leadership involves a lot of time on your part. You still have to live a normal life, however, to keep growing you need to invest significant time to master leadership. You only have so much energy and time to get it all in.

The Pareto principle is a concept used by many businesses in various forms. What we will use it here for is to assess leadership and the leader, you. It works like this, 20 percent of your skills will contribute to 80 percent of your success. If your leadership requires significant hr intervention, the giving difficult interaction and feedback skills would account for 80 percent of your success as a leader. You should be focusing your efforts on the 20 percent of skills and maximizing their potency.

You time is scarce and precious. Build on your strengths, work and identify your weaknesses.

"Excellence is an art won by training and habituation. We do not act rightly because we have virtue or excellence, but we rather have those because we have acted rightly. We are what we repeatedly do. Excellence, then, is not an act but a habit."—Aristotle

124

The Red Slide

You know what you are good at, keep building those foundations so they are unshakeable. They will give you the 80 percent of what you need to succeed. Find the diamonds in the dirt and polish them enough so they are crystal clear. Once you master one diamond go on to the next one. You goal is to master the few skills that you have, while the trivial others are good back ups.

Your knowledge of yourself needs to be transferred into wisdom. Something that you can use. Your leadership will also be built up if you know how to get others to use the Pareto principle for their own skills. More importantly for them to use skills that you do not possess. The Pareto principle operates on less is more. You do not need to have fifty different skills and be good at none of them. Be good at 5 or 6 skills as a leader and you will be great.

To perform this assessment of yourself is a one maybe two person job. You need feedback, both on your past performance. Take a look at your last job interview, how did it go? How could it have gone better if you were better prepared? Do you procrastinate and make small talk instead of working? Do you suffer from analysis paralysis? Whatever the case may be you need to know you.

A final thought from Einstein:

"If you cant explain it simply, You don't understand it well enough."

DEVELOPING STRATEGIC ABILITY

To become a grand master of the 6th century game of Chess takes decades of practice and patience. The game is not merely to play, chess lets you learn about yourself and what your real self assessment is. We often under estimate and more often over estimate our skills. Chess humbly corrects us.

Your control of what you chose to think about is often ,in chess, mismanaged by a love and hate relationship of your feelings and yourself. As a amateur chess player (really amateur) I often catch myself comedically negating inside my head for making a foolish move. The theoretical part of chess is war, where there is life and death, where pawns become queens and where everything depends on the king. Sacrifices must be made in order to complete the game.

Life much like chess engulfs many of its aspects. You and your opponent are going to battle and you are on a death ground situation that if you lose you die. The funny thing is, that you are responsible for success or failure.

The way most people play chess is the way most people live their lives. On their own way. Most are unsuccessful and content with what they are given. Leaders on the other hand, find out what they are doing wrong and work on that area until they master it. Knowing what sacrifices must be made. In chess if your opening is bad you will have a hard time clawing back, much like in leadership. If you do not have the capability to identify what you are doing wrong in a chess game, you are bound to repeat the same mistakes over and over again.

Interestingly enough, most people keep doing the same recipe over and over and think that it will yield more or give better results. Leadership that does not adjust and improve will not stay in the same place but actually degrade and lose effectiveness.

Look at leadership as a partial piece of chess, it is part life, part sport, part art and part science. These elements make a effective leader strive for excellence. We want rules for leadership, we want shortcut methods and calculations that will give us a repeatable recipe, unfortunately it doesn't work this way. We want a dogmatic approach, and if you play with real chess players (not me) you will understand that dogma or set rules of play don't exist; they adjust to you not the game.

"We dont get a chance to do many things, and every one should be really excellent. Because this is our life."—Steve Jobs

To be a grand master, you need to know what is real and what is weakness, even pretend weakness. As each player tries to one up you, you will find yourself guessing if they are setting you up before the slaughter. Leading is much the same, you will have players that envy or despise you and are very well hidden, you will not know they exist, if you are unprepared. Chess like leadership, reading about it wont help you, you must do and act and review and do again.

ENHANCING FOLLOWERS INTO TEAM MEMBERS

Championship teams have world class leaders involved. Both on the field and ones calling the shots from the sidelines. Any sports team that I active today and is winning on a consistent basis have a selected formula. Very simply, they want to be together.

There are however several factors the must happen for teams wanting to be together, even if they do not like each other. Motivations such as big payouts, incentives, promotions, glory and other human desires give people a reason to stick together.

Before we dive into the meat of what it takes to make a great team, we need to look at what bad teams do and why they are unsuccessful.

Bad to worse

Contrary to what many people think it may not always be the leaders fault for a poor team and the members in it. Would you blame a leader who just inherited a bunch of players and the political red tape ties his hands together so that they cannot act. Many managers and leaders fall into this category, they inherit the other persons bad choices and poor quality and need to clean up, thus they have a bad record until they clean it up.

So what does make a bad team worse. The following qualities contribute:

1. Bad communication among teammates. Could you image if in professional sports none of the players were allowed to talk to each other? The same happens in organizational teams, just that they chose not to talk to each other.

2. Too much of one quality. Having just one quality in a team is not good for productivity and innovation. This is evident again in sports, no position is the same, you have centre, power forward, point guard, small forward-each player with a superior style of play and skill than the other, this is what makes the game interesting and amusing. Organizations often rely on one quality or set of skills that people must possess and in this they spell their demise. Variety is key.

> **"The strength of a team is each individual member. The strength of each member is the team."**—Phil Jackson

3. Not defined where they want to go. Or vision. This does not necessarily just involve the leader. How the team absorbs and understands the vision or the game they are playing determines their outcomes. Imagine a ship captain without a guide or map of where they are going. They get lost at sea because they

wander, ending in starvation or pure luck to succeed. The whole team suffers.

4. Incompetence in members. The inability to find and judge incompetence is debilitating to the whole team. If you have people who have no hope then move on with your lives and get rid of them.

If the above qualities are counterproductive then what should you do as a leader to bring out a great team. First surround yourself with people who are smarter than you. The following are some qualities of a team that can succeed:

1. You set the standard. What you do your team does. What you say your team says. It all starts with you. Optimism is the best medicine, even when times are tough and defeat is at your doorstep you still preach victory and move towards the "adjusted" goal.

2. Your whole team knows the plan. You laid out the framework by which others will fill in the blanks. You do not possess their unique skills, however, you know how they will use them and in which part of the plan. This is the key to your leadership, steer the team to where they can succeed.

3. Role identification. Each member of the team knows what their role is and what their set of skills are there to achieve. They have a unique place in the team and that is why they were

chosen by you. If they are not fine tuned yet it is up to you to find and supply training for them, either by you or by outside influence.

4. Training and growth. You see the value in transferring multiple skills among your team members and back at you. You learn while you teach. You use the strengths of certain team members and utilize them to teach the other members of the team. This collaboration can be done by setting the example from your own world into theirs, you do not hide secrets from your team and you teach all you can, so they can teach each other the same.

Realize that much of team performance must come from the leader, you. Your desire to convey the good in team work will depend on how your body language and mood are displayed to the team members. We talked about confidence in the beginning of the book. Are you slouched and grumpy? Giving a impression of "don't talk to me", are you reserved and have nothing to say because of a personal home dispute? Whatever it is your team picks up these cues and adjusts their attitudes accordingly.

I recall when we were transitioning in some changes in the company and this took a massive toll on me and my personal life. My mood was bad, and we had to fire some people, change others, move this and that. Chaos in the change to get it done. My attitude was not the best, I started noticing when the commotion died down and I went back to being "normal", that my team's mood stayed the same and they were doing the same thing I was and behaving like I was to the employees. How could I have been so ignorant and stupid?! I remember telling myself. This is terrible. That was the last time I let change distort my leadership style.

You need to know how to build teams, everyone you decide to include into your team should be for the goal of making them a golden goose for the 'next' guy and the company. Have a golden touch in development and team functionality like King Midas. Everything he touched turned to gold. So you as well need to have the golden touch on people that work in your teams.

A study of a junior hockey team in Finland researched the effectiveness of the above mentioned qualities of a team. Throughout the season they had great success by following the set standards and not deviating from their plans when hard times came (losses). This team building program resulted in the players playing better in games, coaches and players both showing greater enthusiasm and general commitment to the success of the team.

 Team building is important to organizational success, even though many organizations do not give proper direction to how this is to be done, the leader is on his/her own to develop this.

Here is the reality of the future. You will have no choice, as a leader of the future to embrace individualistic desires, the whole is greater than the sum of all the parts, as Aristotle said. Your effective team building skills will be desired (world wide) so why not start practicing today in building a skill that will launch your leadership career. The individual is celebrated for their trail blazing courage, however, the future (mega) innovations will be built by teams. Celebrating the individualism in team settings, individuals set the bar high for anyone who wants to be a maverick by themselves. Often alienating themselves in the process. After seeing this many will not want to go it alone and would appreciate the support of a strong team and leader.

The performance of the team is dependent on the mental status of the leader and the situation they finds themselves in. What this mental status includes is the parts of the problem that the team will face or are facing. Also the larger parts as well such as the environment and organizational pieces that determine the context of team progress. Emphasis on the progress of the leaders ability to move ahead with the team.

The response that you have to this problem that you saw in your head is to be very flexible behaviourally and posses some skills that will accompany the teams needs to get it done. It is important that you do not stick to your ways but to rather adjust to the teams functioning model of how they solve problems, requiring your actions to mesh with theirs.

Patrick Lencioni mentions in his book "the five disfunctions of a team", the quality building trust. This is most likely the most important ingredient in the team force. Building trust takes energy and makes people vulnerable to attacks, sometimes un-wise attacks that leave people stranded on the vulnerability island because they spoke the truth about something and the others didn't. As a leader you need to see the people who are willing to make a effort in building the teams trust by exposing themselves to others.

Imagine if you went to the confessional and told the priest all your sins, then 5 minutes later he comes out and yells to everyone, "Hey! Do you know what Johnny did! Oh my god your gonna love this!", you would most likely renounce your faith. That vulnerability that is given to you is a sign of trust from the person that is showing it. You teams should never be afraid to say, "I was wrong", and "I need help" and "I'm not sure" around each other.

Building trust shouldn't be a monumental task, it depends on your team members and their levels of security. I remember a employee who, whatever you said to her, the answer always was negative. The level of insecurity in people will vary and from there you should adjust your team timing. The method of building trust is to know you team members and they know you, it does take your initiative to get it complete and get it going.

The team members knowing each other is the first step into identifying that everyone is human, and that these humans are part of the mistake making routine. Once everyone accepts

"Im not upset that you lied to me, I'm upset that from now on i cannot believe you."— Friedrich Nietzsche

135

each other as human and not machine, the process for team building can continue.

There are various ways that you can have trust building moments. It might be a routine that you have with your team. On a Monday you make small talk about the weekend and ask about their kids, dog etc. As the leader you know your team listens to you, if they want to follow you is a whole different story. They will follow you if they trust you.

PRESSURE- A CONTEXT TO URGENCY

A serious attempt to achieve results involves the active involvement of the individual or a team of leaders. This change effort to make something out of nothing, where there has been an absence of results requires pressure.

Pressure and stress are interrelated but are not similar. Stress is subjective to the person that is experiencing it. We say we are stressed because we cannot pay our bills, however, to someone who does not view bill paying as stressful, or someone else manages their money (meaning they never see their pay go into bills) paying bills is not stressful for them. Stress is also manageable as the more you are exposed to the same situation you become akin to its behaviour and adapt very quickly relinquishing the stress.

"You cant build a reputation on what you are going to do."–Henry Ford

No, pressure is different and necessary in leadership. There are ways to use pressure properly. Many managers and inexperienced leaders put pressure on others unnecessarily because they do not know any other approach. Everything is 'urgent' to them, they

___

need everything 'now'. This is not leadership or management but bullying.

Pressure in scientific terms is equal to force divided by area. The less of an area the higher the pressure exerted. Imagine pushing the palm of your hand onto your forearm, you feel some pressure, now imagine doing the same thing with your index finger on that same area, the pressure is much greater because it is focused.

The leader has a decision to make, everyday they wake up and engage themselves in their role they must decide on what direction they will be taking their teams. If you are faced with a poor performing team on any level you must decide when, what and how you will deliver pressure you need to give to the team.

When to give pressure-Perfect Timing

To best describe the moment that you should give pressure we should look at the Ronin known as Miyamoto Musashi who wrote the 17th century book "The book of five rings". He says, "There is timing in everything", timing cannot be mastered until it is practiced. You will learn this through trial and error as finding the right time to give and dish out the proper pressure to achieve results will be critical. Too early and nobody will understand why you are doing this, you look foolish too late and you missed the vital time to make changes, you look like a person without a plan.

Miyamoto mentions that timing is like playing music, the proper way to play music is to have rhythm and to do this is in timing. Riding horses, shooting bows and guns, speaking and strategizing all involve timing, many skills demand proper and diligent time management for their own sake.

You must know the cyclical nature of time and life, you have ups and downs and they reflect your decision making abilities. You should discern when you are capable of making decisions or not (see EQ chapter for further explanation). Sometime the moment is not to do anything, with that you do more with inaction than running full steam ahead. Maybe the time is not right to give more pressure or any at all. Let wounds heal.

You know your timing by knowing your enemies timing, of which they are not aware of. Miyamoto's words echo into our leadership practice as well, knowing what your group is going through psychologically and in what state that puts them, either engaged or depressed or surviving gives you a reference point to work from. Acting too soon and putting more pressure on broken bones (layoffs, bad results, project rejections) could further damage the group morale.

All five books of the Master Samurai Swordsman are in some form related to timing. Thinking about when, is mostly strategy and strategic thinking. Planning on what will happen before it happens. Exerting pressure on strategies and plans that are not yet ready for it will impede progress rather than make them better. Charles Darwin after discovering the theory of evolution spent another 8 years building his resume so people would take him seriously, knowing that the time was not yet right for him to emerge and tell the world.

For timing you need to master patience. Observe the effective people around you in your office and other examples throughout history and you will see their iron clad patience. Never in a hurry and never rushed they know exactly what the next move is and when to make it. They spend 8 hours chopping down a tree of which 6 are spent sharpening their axe as Abraham Lincoln used to say.

"Do nothing which is of no use."— Miyamoto Musashi

Accurate timing will prevent you from making moron blunders with your teams. Here is a final list from Miyamoto in timing strategy and how you will use it to decipher pressure in leading:

1. Be honest with yourself

2. Success is embedded in training and practice

3. Do not be a stranger to foreign skills, learn as much as you can

4. Understand all professions

5. In life understand the differences between losses and wins

6. Build your intuition and judgment as well as the understanding for all things

7. See the things that cannot be seen

8. Keep a close eye even on trivial matters

9. Don't waste time

What kind of pressure is right?

When you understand that you NEED to give pressure you need to discern what kind of pressure is needed for the group. Some people call this micromanagement and its been given a bad name over the years. However, in poor performing groups the direct involvement of a leader is not micromanagement rather engagement. It is the leader who is trying to figure out what is going wrong and needs to deep dive in every aspect of the problem.

When you do figure out what the problem is, you need to decide whether it is going to be a palm or a finger amount of pressure. Do you need to focus your efforts on a single piece of the picture exerting all your teams effort on that one part?

When the Romans figured they could not beat Hannibal in battle, they figured they needed to switch their game plan and attack his home base. Forcing him to return, tired and battle worn they would have a final battle at Zama, which he eventually lost and Carthage surrendered to Rome. They focused their effort on a single area not the whole problem (Hannibal at their doorsteps). While Hannibal destroyed the individual armies he faced he could not win the war.

_____

One of the worst things that you can do is not say anything. If you think that your silence will solve the problems that your group is facing you are putting lipstick on a pig and thinking its not a pig. The problem, especially with leadership and new leaders is that they don't say enough and actually not what they say.

One of the main ideas you need to foster before any kind of delivery is, do the people in your group feel safe? Is what you are about to talk about going to hurt anyone, emotionally, professionally, psychologically? If the answer is yes, you need to structure your approach differently. Especially with more stress inducing news you need to let them know that they can reflect on that.

In regards to pressure, often times small problems that could have used a little bit of pressure to get done, didn't. The reason was, is that it wasn't shared with the right people at the right time and it escalated into something much more than it should have. You get blind sided by this out of the blue, thinking that it came out of nowhere when in reality it was building up in pressure for a while.

"I have been impressed with the urgency of doing. Knowing is not enough; we must apply. Being willing is not enough; we must do."— Leonardo Da Vinci

142

The Red Slide

After you feel that your group has the comfort to actually share ideas and thoughts with you, you can approach them with the added news. You are actually being honest and open to them, grounding them in reality and to reality. We are here to do a job and we cant move away until its done, we have this much time to do xyz.

It is not enough if 50% of your group is going to follow through with your plans on making that change or trying to achieve that result. The delivery of the message needs to have accountability involved. Pressure begets more pressure if accountability is not acted on. If only 50% of your team is working towards a solution they will resent the leader for not acting on the other 50% of the team that is on the sidelines.

CLIMBING THE RED SLIDE OF LEADERSHIP

The goal of much study was how to define leadership and leaders. The massive amounts of data that we have today and historical examples and documents that exemplify leaders and their achievements still are not crystal clear on why people choose to be leaders and what make a great leader. This enigma of leading is prevalent in that its mysterious nature is hidden in almost everyone that wants to awaken it.

Machiavelli, Plato, Aristotle, the Bible all have made attempts to define what leadership is. A simple answer to this is, that it just, is. It is a outward calling that people are accidentally called to or deliberately worked on. Leadership is a piece of the human condition, of being alive, we all have varying levels of it in what we do, everyone that is alive today. Anyone who wants to journey and work at it can be a leader in some form.

It is true, however, that not very many can be leaders. The life of leaders is anything but a free ride and easy.

"Expect progress not perfection."— John MacArthur

Do not become delusional that you will have more time if you lead a group of people, you will have less. Do not think that you will catch all of your children's basketball games and attend all parent teacher interviews, you will not. You have a dedicated calling to a group of followers that look to you for answers.

You will not have more time for yourself and your recreational activities as you will spend it fixing other peoples problems that often "you" will take the blame for. You will not have more time for the wife or husband because you will be spending it learning new things, reading , seminars, trainings etc. Your life as a leader might be very lonely, you might be by yourself.

So ask yourself if this is a path you want to go down on? Is the amount of effort really worth a trivial result, that you might not see in months, even years? Is leadership really worth the headaches? Is it worth your health and your family life? Can you live with the mistakes others make and own them for yourself? Are you doing it because of the money not because you truly want to lead? What is your final calling in life....

Almost all the people you talk to in your life will have some excuse why something cannot work and will not happen, and that the sacrifice is not worth the effort. When you enter this world of leading, you commit, to everyone and most of all yourself that you are not backing down for anything or anyone. Your integrity and your values of what is right and what needs to happen are your fuel for success.

Corsican Emperor Napoleon, when he was just a teenager his ability to serve his country gave him the opportunities to prove himself. After the artillery siege of Toulon in 1793 he was promoted to brigadier general at the age of 24. We often find ourselves in positions that we ourselves are not aware of. We do not see our brilliance, but others do and they promote us.

These individuals that see in us a light of leadership has always been with us, only as we experience life and deal with life does this light go stronger. Napoleons light was his ability to learn his craft fast and use it for the service of his country. His success was in the charismatic willingness to be at the front of the battle, often unnecessary, putting himself at personal risk.

"leaders are dealers in hope", as Napoleon liked to say. You are the hope that people look to in order to keep them going. Superhero characters are nothing more than leaders in fancy costumes, they deal hope in all of their stories, Superman saves metropolis, Batman rescues Gotham and so on. Why does the human perception love superhero's? They are not real, but we want them to be so bad. We say to ourselves, if we only had that kind of person here today, he would take care of those problems. We live in a world of hopelessness. Your leadership is pieced by the hopeful wishes of the followers, you took it upon yourself to fill their hopes.

"Do not try to lead men who are unwilling to follow you; if their heart is not in it, you will never find the old spirit or the old courage." — Arrian

As Socrates, you must preserve good and the good life to you followers and yourself, in order to be worthy of the name leader.

Being a follower first

The way we see the world is both conceptual and subjective to our thoughts and experiences. Leadership is not about leading in the end. It is much more than that. Adding more responsibility and stress to you life is not the ideal life. The way in which things appear to us is the way they are, their true form and they cannot be what we imagine them or wish them to be.

All of our worldly experiences can only come to us through our faculties, our sensory-sight, taste, sound, touch, and feeling. It is not what it out there that we experience but the nature of our faculties that we possess, that are our genetic makeup. Our past experiences influence how we will experience new things and strange events that are unknown at that present moment in time. All experience as such is subject dependent, you. You cannot replicate your experience to anyone else on this earth or in history because it is your unique experience.

Leadership is such a faculty that cannot be emulated, replicated, multiplied or osmosis to anyone but yourself. There are two realities, the one which is things/events as they are independent of the experience (science) and to these things we have no access, second-there are things as they appear to us, the world as it comes to our minds through experiences. So we do not dive into time and space or any of that nonsense what we must know now is that we are to follow only in order to lead.

The phenomenon of leadership is just the same as the phenomenon of genetic makeup. We are born, all of us to lead. Our predisposed reality that society lays on you makes you a follower. This is a double negative as to lead you need to follow, and to follow you should lead. One cannot exist without the other. Great leaders have always been followers to a certain degree. You leadership must be stronger in the majority of time than your follower-ship.

It is special to talk about leadership because it is in itself special. No two leaders are alike. The physical world of objects and things can be replicated, even animals can be looked at as a consistent sameness. We humans classify ourselves as sameness beings, however, we are not. Especially in leadership we are not same. Our physical being is what we personally know more than anyone else on this planet, in this physical body we have our uniqueness building for the leadership that we will use. Follower-ship build on this leadership as a mason builds statues, slowly and ever so carefully. We have a 6th sense of this leadership building only made possible by the years of following and only made possible by our own acknowledgement of the emerging leader in us.

Most of your life you have followed, and the vast majority of people will always follow because of their underdeveloped faculties towards leadership. You have made a breakthrough, and are following through towards the premise that your reality is leading others. Like many philosophers have said, our own motivations towards this leadership and of leading are unknown to us and are made unconsciously. We do not know what exactly motivates us, but we stay motivated, that we are unconscious of our own inner selves. This explains the reality that leaders work longer, stay later and experience more joy when others are beaten. They don't know how to describe this feeling but they know it exists, and they cannot replicate it but want more of it.

To have leadership made real. Reality being that it exists and there is knowledge of it, there must be followers. Knowledge is a result of time, time is of our world whereas space is not. For follower and leader to exist there must exist knowledge of one another, if one does not exist the other does not. This is the premise of following. You to be a leader, you must be a follower, and to be a follower you must be a leader. Reality of the premise of existence of one another.

You cannot be indifferent in the pursuit of leadership. Both negative and positive aspects must be looked at and self taught. In order to learn total leadership you need to understand from, foundation to roof, of leading.

www.ingramcontent.com/pod-product-compliance
Lightning Source LLC
Chambersburg PA
CBHW051919170526
45168CB00001B/458